Perfectly Positive
How To Stay Positive When Life Is Not Perfect

SaBrina Fisher Reece

Copyright 2024 by SaBrina Fisher Reece
Los Angeles, California
All rights reserved.
Printed and bound in the United States of America
Published And Distributed by
Impact Publishing
Los Angeles, California

In59Seconds@yahoo.com
Packaging/Consulting
Professional Publishing House
1425 W. Manchester Ave. Ste B
Los Angeles, California 90047
323-750-3592
Email: professionalpublishinghouse@yahoo.com
www.ProfessionalPublishingHouse.com

Cover Design & Concept: SaBrina Fisher Reece @in59secs
Graphic art created by: Joshua Sims @jsimsgraphics
First printing
978-1-7365592-2-2 (paperback)
978-1-7365592-3-9 (hardcover)

No part of this book may be reproduced, stored in a retrieval system, or transmitted in any form or by any means without the prior written permission of the author and publisher, except by a reviewer who may quote brief passages in a review to be printed in a newspaper, magazine, or journal. For inquiry, contact the author at: In59Seconds@yahoo.com

Dedication

I specifically dedicate this book to my two youngest daughters, Jayden Charlee and Journey Schy, and my grandsons, Raiden Jesse and Rio Jordan. I love you all so very much. I will always be with you.

You all will live and grow up in a world vastly different from your ancestors. Please remember that no matter how challenging the world may be, happiness and peace can exist. You can experience a wonderful life if you remember the control you have over it. The concept of "Perfectly Positive" does not mean you have to be a perfect person. Nor does it mean you won't make mistakes throughout your lives. Instead, it aims to teach you the daily tools needed to navigate each situation and find the positive solution.

The title, "Perfectly Positive," is a reminder to stop, breathe, and think first in all situations. The primary goal is to prove to you that doing so will lead you to the ideal action and response. The response that is perfect for you. The response that allows you to lead with love and compassion for yourself and others, uplifting and encouraging everyone, and evoking peace and happiness for all. Mind is All, and everything begins and ends in your mind. You can accomplish everything you desire if you hold strong to the belief that you can. Your thoughts are like crayons; use them to color a beautiful life.

About the Author

SaBrina Fisher Reece is a creative author, artist, and entrepreneur. Above all, she is a dedicated mother of four and a loving "Grammie" to two grandsons. She is passionate about making a positive impact on the world and is committed to sharing the transformative tools she has utilized in her own personal transformation journey with future generations.

Her first book, *My Spiritual Smile: Tools for Mental and Emotional Transformation*, recounts her traumatic past and provides readers with the methods she used to heal from abandonment and childhood tragedy. Her second book, *Your Mind Is Magic*, which she considers her masterpiece, emphasizes that the mind is powerful and must be controlled, or it will control us. We have the power to master our thoughts and Manipulate Ideas in a New Positive Direction.

When SaBrina isn't writing self-help books, she is teaching sound meditation classes at A New Vision Studio in Los Angeles or giving dynamic motivational speeches to audiences of men, women, and children, reminding them that anything is possible if they believe in themselves. **@SoundWithSaBrina www.SoundWithSaBrina.com**

Her spiritual art collection, titled "Spiritual Art From My Heart," reflects a passion for painting that she rekindled in her fifties.

www.SpiritualArtFromMyHeart.com
@SpiritualArtFromTheHeart

During her transformation journey, SaBrina created the **#In59Seconds Movement.** This movement aims to teach others how to uplift, motivate, and encourage themselves and others. Its primary mission is to remind individuals that they hold the key to their own happiness. It focuses on training them to emerge from darkness and recognize they are worthy of all the beautiful things life has to offer.

Table of Contents

Introduction 1

Chapter 1:
Positivity Is Not Perfect 3

Chapter 2:
Our Daily Bread 11

Chapter 3:
*How to Stay Positive Throughout the
    Disappointments in Life* 40

Chapter 4:
Be Intentional 85

Chapter 5:
Imagine the Best 98

Chapter 6:
Mastering Detachment 109

Chapter 7:
Live for Yourself 128

Chapter 8:
When "Just Go Pray About It" Is Not Enough 140

Chapter 9:
Vibrate High 146

Chapter 10:
You Win The War–The World is Yours 166

INTRODUCTION

Perfectly Positive will not only emphasize the importance of thinking positively but how to sustain those thoughts daily. It will show you how to choose not to suffer throughout your day, even when faced with minor challenges.

You will learn to find the positive in all situations and maintain a healthy state of mind.

Many things can anger and annoy us during the day. It is essential to recognize those emotions and change them instantly. Allowing ourselves to stay upset, sad, frustrated or annoyed is dangerous. Negative emotions will increase if not reversed. Throughout life, there will always be highs and lows, but you are in control. You are the master of your own fate, and you have the power to make good out of bad.

You will learn to navigate daily situations at home, work, and in everyday life that prevent you from being positive. While some incidents are undeniably negative and impactful, it's also crucial to identify smaller daily situations that contribute to a negative mindset. These tiny day-to-day instances are like logs tossed into a raging fire, fueling negative emotions and lowering our vibrational frequency. You must identify and extinguish them.

This book will teach you to develop the practice of putting out those small mental and emotional fires, preventing them from merging into a massive destructive force within you. Being positive does not mean being perfect. It's simply a daily barometer we set for ourselves, allowing us to experience the best this earthly life has to offer.

CHAPTER 1

Positivity Is Not Perfect

There is absolutely nothing perfect about being positive. It's hard and requires focus and endurance. Positivity is a learned behavior and must become second nature to be maintained. This book will teach you practical skills on how to be and stay positive, no matter what's happening in your life. Life happens to us all, and it's not always filled with happy, wonderful moments. We must learn how to navigate the harder times and not let them consume us mentally. While we cannot control everything that happens in the world around us, we can learn to control how we think.

One thing I like to remind myself is that even though many negative situations actually exist in our lives in real time, more than half of them only exist in our minds. We often fear negative circumstances that never actually happen. We think hundreds of negative thoughts daily, not realizing the damage these thoughts alone can cause. We fear pain, sadness, failure, heartbreak, and more. Allowing those fears to occupy the majority of our mind space can prevent us from enjoying this amazing world.

First, we need to develop tools to immediately recognize negative thoughts and then stop ourselves from thinking them in order to eliminate the mental chaos. Next, we must learn to empower ourselves mentally and emotionally. We can take full control of our thinking patterns and replace all negative thoughts with positive ones. Negative thoughts are garbage that we must discard. They can't stay around because they will grow and take over your mind. Negative thoughts are the internal enemy and we must treat them as such. You can't hang out with them, touch them, or look them in the face and converse with them. This enemy is unseen, but is the most important enemy of them all. Negative thoughts must go! They mean absolutely no good and must be eliminated.

Only you can rid yourself of a negative thinking pattern. No one can do it for you. This book provides ideas and tools, but you have to be committed to doing the work yourself. The work I speak of may be taxing at times, and you may want to give up, but please don't. The reward for changing a negative thinking pattern into a positive one is priceless. Changing your mindset and learning how to maintain a positive state of mind will be one of the best decisions you ever make. That one decision alone will drastically improve your quality of life.

Once I realized I controlled the suffering that negative thoughts brought me, my quality of life changed for the better. Recognizing my power to eliminate negative thoughts allowed me to create a better life for myself where I didn't have to remind myself of every perceived flaw. I don't have to relive my past trauma, and neither do you. Past trauma is just that—past. It's not happening to you now. You don't have to keep reviving and bringing it back to life in your mind. Stop the self-torment and realize that you have been the tormentor, choosing to continue negative thinking. You are the one driving the bus.

I'm not saying it is easy to let go of the horrible, painful experiences of the past. I have had my share of tragic events, too. The injustices you may have endured are valid. However, you do not have to suffer from the effects forever. No matter how hard it is to let it go, it is vital to do so if you want to live a wonderful life. You must release the anger and resentment that may still linger. Holding on to anger, hurt, and resentment doesn't hurt others; it hurts ourselves.

I was an abandoned child and suffered many childhood traumas because of my mother's drug addiction. However, right now, in the present moment, I am not living through those situations—they are in my past. But every time I thought of them, I experienced their pain again. I would mentally relive the devastation of the events, causing myself the pain and hurt.

It's a difficult concept to teach others, but continuously thinking about past abuse, hurt, and pain is a choice. We can stop those thoughts. We can say, "Nope, not today," and push those thoughts right out of our heads. Yes, they will return, but we must be consistent. We can choose to focus only on positive thoughts. When negative thoughts come, acknowledge them first, because you cannot change what you are in denial about. We cannot heal what we hide. Acknowledge the negative emotions and thoughts, then cast them out and replace them with positive options.

Imagine memories as if they are videos. You don't have to keep replaying them or rewinding to watch again. Stop replaying negative memories and focus on moving forward in your life. It's the only way to a bright and happy future. Everyone deserves a happy and positive life, but first we must believe it is possible.

Many people ask me, "How do you stay so positive?" I don't wake up feeling positive every day. For example, if I wake up in a negative space, I immediately start using the tools I've learned to help me return to a positive headspace. I'll share the tools that work best for me, but you will need to find those that work best for your life. I firmly believe in having practical tools to maintain a positive state of mind. Try out a few different tools to see which fit well into your life. Choose tools and practices that you believe in wholeheartedly and are more likely to sustain.

To stay positive, I use the following tools:

1. **Positive Affirmations**

    Speaking positive statements aloud to myself. For example:
    - I am beautiful.

- I am happy.
- I am successful.
- My business is a great success.
- I am worthy of love.
- I am in great health.
- My life is peaceful.
- Money flows easily and frequently into my life.

2. Creative Visualization

Learn to create a visual image in your head. Picture yourself in the new home you desire or sitting at the desk of that new job you feel you deserve. Visualize your magical wedding day to the partner who possesses all the qualities you desire. Close your eyes and create the images in your mind's eye. If it's a car you desire, see that car in your mind. Picture the specific details: the color of the exterior and interior, the seats, and dashboard color. Imagine yourself gratefully driving around, hands on the steering wheel. Remember, everything that exists was a picture in someone's mind first.

3. Meditation

Learning to be still is one of the best tools I have ever learned. Simply sitting in a quiet place and breathing. Most of us are too busy with the hustle and bustle of life to just sit still and focus on our breathing patterns. As simple as it seems, it's not. It requires focus and discipline. Our mind speaks to us all day, but we are too busy to hear it. Once we learn the art of being still, only then can we notice when we are having negative thoughts. In order to change negative thoughts into positive ones, we first have to notice they are there. You can't change something until you acknowledge its existence. Meditation allows you the quiet time needed to recognize the things you need to change.

4. Mirror Work

Mirror work is priceless and unbelievably effective. Just stand in front of a mirror and speak the affirmations you created aloud, as I suggested in #1. Look at yourself and say uplifting things repeatedly until you believe them. The DNA cells in your body can actually hear you, so be repetitive and consistent. Repeating powerful, encouraging words is like planting seeds in a garden. Eventually, they will grow, just like plants in a garden. The constant repetition is like water; without it, the things we plant die. Similarly, without reinforcing affirmations, our mind and body won't accept the new thoughts. We must repeat them until we truly believe them. This will allow us to generate the feelings needed to manifest them into our lives.

5. Reading

I write books because reading books changed my life. Reading stories of perseverance and determination showed me I do not have to identify as a victim for the rest of my life. I have survived a few tragedies, and books gave me hope that the pain would eventually cease. Reading allowed me to see different perspectives and taught me I didn't have to accept every thought as fact. It revealed my inner power and my ability to be happy despite early childhood traumas. The same applies to each of you. Reading helped me view the world differently and understand the importance of balance. Good and bad will always exist, but books helped me realize that light will eventually emerge from the darkness. I read every chance I get and will continue writing books for as long as I live. Books and the vast knowledge within them are essential to our mental and spiritual growth.

6. Grounding/Earthing

There is value in taking time to plant your feet directly in the soil. Walking on grass or untreated concrete grounds us and connects us with the natural properties of the Earth. It's something I didn't learn until my fifties, and I truly wish I had known about it earlier in life. We are so conditioned to covering our feet with shoes that the idea of going barefoot rarely occurs to us. Our amazing Mother Earth possesses powerful healing properties, and research has proven that going barefoot offers numerous health benefits. Planting our feet in the grass or on uncoated concrete can help our bodies heal from various ailments. Sometimes, conventional medicine doesn't seem to work, and we have nothing to lose by walking in nature. Why not? Many of us are wary of man-made medicine, which often has side effects. I'm not suggesting anyone stop taking their medication, but there is no harm in incorporating practices that allow you to reconnect with nature.

7. Stillness

"Be still and know that I am God" (Psalms 46:10). The older you get, the more you understand the importance of stillness. Simply shutting down the mouth and mind and sitting quietly gives you a chance to observe and process the present moment. As I age, this practice becomes increasingly valuable to my life. Every morning, your body may not feel at its best, but taking a few minutes to sit in stillness and breathe will help ensure a better start to the day's journey.

CHAPTER 2

Our Daily Bread

In Matthew 6:11, the reference of daily bread is referring to substance for the body. However, I view positive thinking as equally important as the food needed to sustain nourishment of the human body. Daily we must eat to live. Daily, we should also nourish our minds to live a good life. Once you fully accept that your thoughts manifest your reality and take accountability for the negative circumstances in your life, you'll understand the significance of maintaining a positive mindset. It's detrimental to your life experience here on earth.

In this chapter, I detail small daily situations that cause us to have negative thoughts and how to navigate through them and return to a positive place. While it's easy to identify major chaos and catastrophes in our lives, it's the small daily situations that cause us the most stress and hinder our ability to remain positive. The phrase "What you think about, you bring about" is a principle I live by. Your predominant thoughts become your reality. It's as simple as that. Think about death, doom, and gloom, and you will not experience a life of love, good health, and happiness. It's just like food: eat good, healthy food that nourishes your body, and your body will operate at optimal potential. Similarly, think good, uplifting, positive thoughts daily and on purpose, and your life will become a direct reflection of those thoughts.

The first fact you should learn to accept is that "Your thoughts create your reality." Developing an unshakable belief in this will help you understand the importance of controlling your thoughts. If you don't believe your thoughts influence your life, you are less likely to prioritize thought monitoring. Many of our fears are thoughts we create in our minds—fear of loss, fear of death, fear of failure are all emotions that we first think and then feel. Stop for a second and recall the last time you had a fearful thought. Most likely, it wasn't a verbal exchange with another person but an internal conversation with yourself. We say things to ourselves daily, often horrible things that others would never say to us. We insult and belittle ourselves continuously, becoming our own worst enemies.

I designed this book to help us stop the negative self-talk and remember that we are perfect just as we are. Being intentional about our self-talk is a step toward mastering positive thinking, even in a world filled with negativity.

I understand the idea of having to regulate your thoughts daily may sound exhausting, but once it becomes a habit, it won't be as taxing. When you fully grasp the dangers of not controlling your thinking patterns, you will indeed want to be in control of them. This control gives power over your life and allows you to be *"Perfectly Positive"* in an imperfect world. You will find joy in designing your own destiny. The notion that life happens to you and you have no control over it will fade away. It will become clear that you are in charge of how your life turns out.

Knowing that your thoughts can bring you happiness, prosperity, great health, peace, and love is empowering. You can have all these things, but first, you must learn to stay positive. Staying positive does not mean you are oblivious to the surrounding negativity. It means that even when faced with negativity, you are still in control. During those times, you learn the tools to keep your mind from sinking into a dark, negative spiral. The longer you stay in that dark space, the more darkness and negative energy you attract into your life.

I must reiterate: it is not easy. If you are not used to positive thinking, you will have to rearrange how you think. Many people are classic pessimists. We all know those "woe is me" people who find fault in everything and rarely see their blessings. It will be harder for them, but even they can accomplish this transformation, and it will change their lives for the better.

The key is not to delude yourself into thinking negative things don't and won't happen. They will always exist. You must learn how to react to them positively. No matter how bad things are, you must learn to return to a positive state of mind. For example, if you lose your job unexpectedly, and you might instantly feel angry, scared, and resentful. You may wallow in self-pity and want to scream, "The world is unfair!" I am not telling you to suppress those feelings; just don't stay in that negative space. Use the tools from this book to return to a positive mindset. Start speaking positive affirmations like "I am very talented and many companies want to hire me," or "I have many job opportunities to choose from." Use visualization techniques to imagine yourself at your new job, picturing the office space and positive interactions with co-workers. The objective is to let these mental images generate positive feelings. Just like magic, it's yours, but you have to do the work, and that work always begins with a positive thought.

If you are having trouble identifying negative thoughts, they look and feel like this: You walk into the gym and suddenly feel fat, thinking people are looking at you and saying, "She is here regularly but never seems to lose a pound." No one has said this to you, and you have no proof anyone feels this way. This is all in your head. You made it up. They simply waved and smiled, and you formed this negative narrative. So who suffers? Yes, only you. They are busy living in their self-created world. In times like these, you must master casting out that negative story and replacing it with a positive one. Change that narrative to something that makes you feel wonderful about yourself. Tell yourself people are glancing your way and smiling because they like you and find you very attractive. This is your world—why create pain? Create a world where people love and adore you and your company. Create a world that produces good, secure feelings daily.

Positive thinking is just as important as food—our daily bread. Our bodies need it, and our mind needs it. Without it, we live a dark life of lack and limitation. People who can't think positively unfortunately live a pessimistic life. They believe they have no control and must accept everything that comes their way. That is not the truth. While there are situations, especially in childhood, that seem beyond your control, once you learn to take control of your mind and manage your thinking patterns, you no longer have to suffer from anything that has ever happened to you. You no longer have to relive the horrible trauma of the past. You can invoke happy feelings every day. You can summon prosperity and good health into your life.

This is precisely why I wrote this book. I want everyone to know that this is not a horrible world. Although horrible things happen, we can still be happy. We can choose to find the positive in every situation. When I was younger, I never believed that. I thought I had suffered so much that I was destined to live a life of sadness and depression. I was wrong. I applied the very tools I teach in this book to my own life. I went from a hopeless, suicidal young woman to the dynamic salon owner, a peaceful sound meditation teacher (www.SoundWithSaBrina.com), an author of many best selling self help books, a spiritual artist (@SpiritualArtFromTheHeart), and a phenomenal motivational speaker. Those opportunities exist for everyone. No matter what you have been through, all things are truly possible. You just have to get your mind right first.

Frequently, I use the phrase "Mind is all! It's also a chapter title in my first book "My Spiritual Smile" Everything begins in the mind, from the laptop I am typing on right now to the table it rests on. These objects were all thoughts and ideas in the mind of a human being first. All feelings are mental; you can't physically see feelings. When you are sad, it is your mind that tells you so. When you are happy, you can't see that either. Happy people do not emit some visible happiness mist as they walk by. It's an unseen emotion, just like sadness. You and others can see the physical actions you take when feeling these emotions, but the emotions themselves are invisible. The mind is the source of good and bad things. When we have feelings of inadequacy or fear, these are products of the mind. Since the mind controls so much, we must learn to command authority over it and stop letting it control us.

Once you start paying attention, you will find many opportunities throughout your day to practice controlling your mind. It can be small situations. For example, one day I was at my salon, and my client was not only late but also $20 short with his payment. Initially, it annoyed me. As I stood behind him doing his hair, I had an attitude because he knew my rules and he had made the appointment over a month prior, giving him plenty of time to ensure he had all the money. This is precisely one of the daily situations I want you to learn how to master after reading this book. These are perfect times to change negative thoughts into positive ones.

I reminded myself that this man had been a loyal client for over six years. I told myself that I was going to accept the $20 loss this one time and not be upset about it. To do this, I had to shift into a mindset of gratitude. It took a moment, and I kept flipping back and forth for a while, but eventually, I decided I would not stand there for four hours mad, especially over $20, when God had blessed me with so much.

By this time in my life, I had done enough transformational work to know the dangers of staying angry. If I stayed mad, I wouldn't be hurting the client; I would be hurting myself. No matter how minimal it may seem, allowing myself to stay upset and work in an atmosphere where I'm annoyed and resentful for four hours is suffering. Suffering of any kind causes sickness and disease. It lowers our vibrational frequency, opening the door for more negative things to happen. This is creating "hell" for yourself while on earth.

Even if the client never knew I was upset, I knew, my body knew, and my mind knew. The frequency I was emitting was not high and happy; it was low because of my attitude. Believe it or not, others can feel low frequency or attitude. Holding on to a negative attitude and having negative internal dialogue for an extended period is dangerous for the mind, body, and soul.

So, on this day, while the client was still in my chair, I had a conversation with myself. I said, "SaBrina, God has blessed you with so much. Today you will gladly take this $20 loss and you will not make the customer feel bad about it. You will take a deep breath and remember that he has never done this before and remind yourself in this moment to be kind and loving." I also reminded myself how financially blessed I had been to own a hair salon for twenty-six years consistently. Once I talked to myself, I was able to relax, release my frustration, and peacefully enjoy the next four hours of doing his hair. This is how you navigate a negative situation. Start with yourself. Talk positively to yourself. Change how you choose to view the situation, and you will bring peace to yourself and all involved.

Situations like these happen to us all regularly throughout our day. Use them as growth opportunities. Practice finding the positive in each situation. Practice showing love for yourself and others. Learn to have an internal conversation with yourself and decide that you will not suffer. You will not be mad. You will not let it annoy you, even when those feelings may be justified. Staying in that negative place will only hurt you and hinder your mental and emotional growth.

When we go inside and deal with our inner self first, we are choosing to tap into the God within us. When we listen to those negative voices in our heads and react, we create momentary "hell" for ourselves. Hell is an unhealthy state of mind that we do not have to operate in. Choose to create "heaven" for yourself instead and enjoy this amazing life experience to the fullest.

Here is another example. I spoil my kids. I am not in denial about that at all. I typically spare no expense where they are concerned. However, I still teach them about being grateful, and I am annoyed and disappointed when they display moments of selfishness.

One day, my daughter asked me for an additional $80 after a weekend of entertaining them with expensive tickets to a show and eating at restaurants. She offered to do additional chores around the house for the extra money, which was great because she wasn't so spoiled that she asked for the money without offering to work for it. I thought of some extra household chores, brought home the money, and gladly gave it to her.

As I was coming into the house, I told myself, "Don't give her the money until she has fully completed the chores." I didn't listen to my own advice and because I was tired. I handed her the money while she was still mopping the floor. She said, "Thank you," and I reminded her that she needed to sweep the floor before she mopped it. Noticing that she didn't sweep first gave me an attitude.

My home is a place of peace, so anyone having an attitude disrupts that peace. I address and dismiss all situations that have even the slightest potential of destroying our peaceful home. When I allowed myself to have this attitude with my daughter for not completing her chore thoroughly, I had to remind myself that I knew better than to give her the money before she was done. Yet, I gave her the money early so I could lay down and rest.

Accepting this responsibility caused my attitude to soften with her, because I didn't have to do it. That was my fault. I knew I needed to make sure she completed her chores properly before I handed her the money, but I didn't, so I can only be upset with myself, not her. She is a great, responsible young woman, but she is quite spoiled and entitled. All of my children were spoiled. That is my fault as well.

This is a self-check tool that helps me to take a breath, assess the situation, learn the lesson it presents, and let it go. Rather than suffer with internal anger, which causes headaches, sickness, and lowers your overall vibration. If I didn't check myself for that situation, the rest of my day would have been filled with negative thoughts of *She is an ungrateful brat. Next time she asks, I will say no. She doesn't appreciate me and how hard I work.*

This situation may seem small, but these are exactly the things that happen to us throughout the day that keep us from staying positive. Hence the title of the chapter, "Our Daily Bread." These are the smaller daily situations that keep our minds occupied, even when we don't realize it.

We must always stop first and see what we could have possibly done to get a better outcome. Even if it is not our fault, we still have to make an internal choice not to be upset and move forward in peace. If we want to live in peace, we must intentionally create peace for ourselves. No one is going to do it for us.

My daughter is a great, loving, and generous person. Who does a magnificent job keeping the home clean, giving me more time to work longer hours. It would be unfair to judge her as a whole when she is a little less thorough. We all have unique personality traits, many of which other people may not like. We would not want people to judge us as a whole by the parts of us we need to improve upon. We must be careful in doing that to others.

Every one of us could use some improvement in some area of our lives. When you make it a point to solely focus on the parts of that person that you don't like, you rob yourself of the beautiful parts of them. We are all here to learn and grow. If you were to ask anyone's family members to list facets of their personality, the answers won't be all good or all bad. There is beauty and balance in us all.

The more love and compassion we show to each other, the negative traits you don't like in them seem to disappear. We learn to love them unconditionally. Those other traits don't actually disappear unless they change them; we are just consumed with love and seeing the best in them that we no longer notice.

I want to provide you with as many examples as I possibly can so you become an expert at identifying a negative thinking pattern and a master at changing it. Recognizing when you are thinking negatively is crucial to changing your thoughts. Negative thoughts will continue to come throughout your life. You can't get rid of them entirely, but you can learn how to reject them immediately. The key is to acknowledge, address, and dismiss them on the spot. The longer you allow them to float around inside your mind, the greater the risk of manifesting them into reality. You want the positive thoughts to materialize, not the negative ones. Systematically replacing negative thoughts with positive ones will change your life tremendously. Let's all become *"Perfectly Positive"* so we, and the generations that follow, can live in a better world where everyone is productive, happy, and vibrating high.

When dealing with people on a daily basis, circumstances can sometimes lead us to form negative thoughts about them based on isolated incidents. They may be good people, but because they behaved a certain way on one particular occasion, we allow ourselves to judge them as a whole.

For example, have a friend who has accomplished a lot in life. There was a time when she wasn't making good choices and she lost everything because of it. It took years, but eventually, she put her life back together and regained all she had lost and more. Sometimes, I would tell her how proud I was of her, and I noticed she would never respond or say, "Thank you." When I would allow negative thoughts to creep into my mind. I would say to myself, "She is so rude.

Perfectly Positive

I keep attempting to encourage her and she won't even say anything." She would completely dismiss the compliments. I kept doing it because it's in my nature to uplift others, but I felt like this person was very impolite. This negative thought may have not been true.

I told myself I would not compliment her anymore, which is also negative and the opposite of my true nature. One day, I was heading to a meeting where she would be present. Suddenly, I had a revelation: maybe she isn't responding because she doesn't feel like she deserves the compliment. When people have self-worth issues, no matter what they have accomplished, they still don't feel worthy. At that moment, it seems God needed me to consider a different perspective on why she wasn't saying "Thank you" or acknowledging my attempt to uplift her. Seeing it from that point of view allowed me to be more understanding and decide not to expect a response. I decided I would continue to encourage her, and I reminded myself that I used to do a form of that, too. I too would dismiss compliments when I did not feel worthy of them.

When I started gaining weight and didn't feel at my best, people complimented me, saying, "You look great in that dress." I would say, "Thank you, but I'm clearly not a size 5 anymore." I couldn't accept the compliment and leave it at "Thank you." I had to point out my weight gain, even though they didn't. God had to remind me of that, which allowed me to have more compassion for my friend when she did it.

This is how we change negative thoughts into positive emotions. My friend meant no harm. I find it effortless to compliment others. However, many people do not, and it's even harder for them to receive a compliment. Many people have an abundance of self-worth issues. Some people have never been hugged or encouraged as a child. It may take time, but I find that love and consistency can fix all of that. Love always wins.

There are so many daily instances where we cause ourselves to suffer, often without realizing it. Small situations can lead to unnecessary suffering if we aren't mindful. For example, I have a couple of close friends whom I consider sisters. One morning, I texted one of them to ask about her outfit. She kindly responded, and before ending the conversation, I said, "I love you, sis. Have a great day." She replied with, "You, too, sis," but didn't say "I love you" back.

In moments like these, we can easily get our feelings hurt by assuming the worst. Maybe the "You, too, sis" meant both "Have a great day" and "I love you, too." Initially, I allowed myself to feel a little hurt. I'm positive she loves me and meant no harm. However, when we let our thoughts run rampant, we can indeed perceive a situation in a way that was never intended. I had to do the inner work to realize I was overreacting. She moved on with her day, while I allowed myself to feel hurt over an imagined slight.

The pain I felt when I thought she intentionally didn't say "I love you" back was a choice I made to suffer in that moment. It was me deciding the worst and reacting to it. It was an old, past trauma of "No one loves me" trying to creep up. It's very possible she simply overlooked it or her response of "You too, sis" was meant to cover the sentiment. Or she simply may not be a verbal "I love you" person, and that's okay, too.

Recognizing these times is how we heal ourselves and stop allowing our mind and thoughts to operate in the negative. There will be enough actual situations in life that warrant hurt feelings. We don't have to make up any extra ones and unnecessarily torment ourselves.

Therefore, I named this chapter "Our Daily Bread.'. We need mental nourishment daily. We must learn daily tools to shift our mindset into a positive place. All day long, we have to make conscious choices to return to a positive way of thinking. When choosing the title for this book, I wanted to clarify that life is not perfect. However, when faced with all the challenges, we can strive to be *"Perfectly Positive."*

Do I mean to never make mistakes or never have bad thoughts? Absolutely not. What I am saying is that in each situation, no matter how bad it may seem, attempt to find the positive in it. It may take a while to see it. I completely understand that. But with the belief that "all things work out for the good," as your life unfolds, you will see that there is indeed something positive you can take away from all situations.

If you were once poor, that experience taught you to be more mindful of your finances and gave you a stronger drive for success because you understand what it's like to lack what you need. If you were in a car accident but lived to tell the story, that incident could have made you a more cautious driver, potentially saving lives in the future. If you went through a painful divorce and vowed never to love again, when your heart mends, you will pull lessons from that relationship and apply them to the next one, increasing your chances of a happy, long-lasting relationship.

Apply all life lessons and grow from them. Initially, with a broken heart, you may not see any positive lessons in the situation, but as time goes on, you will gather what you learned, apply it to your future, and move forward. Trust me when I tell you, there is indeed something positive in all situations.

Remember, I use the word "perfect" in this book not to pressure you into perfection, not because we don't have human flaws and make mistakes, but because we are all perfect creations of God even with our perceived flaws. Once we accept and love ourselves, we open our lives to the extreme greatness inside of us all. I use the word "perfect" loosely. No human is without flaws. The goal of this book is to train you to seek the more favorable option in all situations. Try harder in every instance to see the positive.

When you are mad, if you stop, breathe, and think first, you might respond in a way that is helpful, not hurtful, to the situation. When you are hurt or disappointed, please don't respond to anything or anyone until you stop, take a few deep breaths, and internally ask yourself, "What should I do or say to get the best outcome?" Anger is never the answer. Anger is a low-vibrational response. If you respond out of anger, you will invoke more low-vibrational emotions in yourself and others. It's not always easy, but choose love, patience, and kindness; it will definitely pay off in the end.

There was another key incident at my home where I had to aggressively seek peace because I was becoming severely annoyed daily. Sometimes, you have to address a person directly about what's bothering you, but I suggest you never do that when you are angry. Wait until you are in a peaceful state of mind before approaching them.

My next-door neighbors had a cement flower pot that sat very close to my driveway. It was literally at the back corner of my car, and I had to be mindful every day when backing out of my driveway not to hit it. I did that for about a month or two, but eventually, I became resentful and started to say things like, "Why the heck would they place this pot so close to my driveway? They must be trying to irritate me." They may not have even considered the inconvenience it was to me. The thought of irritating me could have been the farthest thing from their minds. This is how we create drama in our heads that may not even be true.

As time went on, I was really getting agitated every time I pulled into and out of my own driveway. This is suffering!

This is a disruption of one's peace. This causes harmful physical symptoms and negative mental thoughts. Finally, I couldn't take it anymore and I texted my neighbor, saying, "Hey, guys, I hope you are having a great day. I'm not the best driver in the world. Please, if you don't mind, can you move the vase over a few feet so that I don't have to worry about hitting it every time I come and go?" They responded immediately, and the next time I came outside, the flowerpot had been moved several feet. That morning stress was gone, and my relationship with my neighbors was not damaged.

In situations where you have to address someone, wait until you are not angry and always lead with respect and love.

Sadly, our own children can cause us deep pain. We would like to think someone we brought into the world could never and would never cause us pain. Well, life is just not that ideal. Our children can hurt us, too. It's not always intentional; they don't know all the things their parents have been through. They have the ability to tap into and open wounds that we possibly didn't know we still hadn't healed.

By age fifty-four, my youngest child, Journey, was ten years old. Along with another family, we planned a big birthday extravaganza for the two birthday girls. Penny, the daughter of the other family, turned thirteen on October 6, and Journey turned eleven on October 18. We had a four-day staycation together. We rented suites at a hotel, had a Spiderman-themed party for them, and took them to a Medieval Times Dinner and Tournament. They had a blast.

Perfectly Positive

One day, while we were just chilling at the hotel, the kids asked my older daughter and me to judge a dance contest for them as we had the day before. Initially, the request annoyed me, because my daughter and I were attempting to take a nap, and the kids burst into the room, jolting us awake to judge their dance battle. However, we got up and did as they asked.

The next day, during a few hours of downtime, I asked the girls if I could teach them a simple four-count cheerleader routine since I saw them practicing cheerleading moves in the hotel's hallway. I was excited about it. I used to be the captain of the varsity cheerleading team in high school. So the idea of teaching them some old moves thrilled me. They said yes, but when I went into my room for a second to get something, they all ran and hid under the tables as if my teaching them a cheer routine was the worst idea ever. It instantly hurt my feelings. I was so hurt that I knew immediately that the source of the pain was not just about their rejection, but that it had triggered some other deep internal feelings within me—feelings of rejection that were not fully healed yet.

I know they are just kids, and in no way do I blame them for their little selfish hurtful actions, but I talked to them about always taking responsibility for how they make others feel. I reminded them of how I was trying to sleep and did not feel like getting up and judging their little dance battle the day before, but I did it for them. It's important that I teach my children about owning how they treat others and make them feel. Aside from the unexpected teachable moment that situation gave me, I realized inside of me there was an unhealed deeper issue with rejection that the smaller incident with the children ripped the bandage off of. There was more work to be done.

So, although the little girls hurt my feelings, I am grateful that the incident happened because it made me aware that I am not fully healed from my childhood feelings of abandonment and rejection. For that revelation, I am grateful. You can't fix something if you are not aware it needs fixing. Often, we push our unhealed wombs deeply inside of us. We mask them, and they never get attended to. The tiniest of things can trigger them, and others many never understand. They may accuse you of overreacting. It truly is not anyone's issue but yours. We have to take the initiative to heal from all of our own mental and emotional wounds. That is one of the key reasons I write books and share with others how I healed mine. Healing is indeed possible for everyone.

I shared that story to illustrate how the smallest of circumstances can highlight our deepest wounds. We must use these daily encounters to practice being "*Perfectly Positive.*" This doesn't mean being a perfect person, void of human faults and mistakes. It means recognizing the greatness within us and applying it to every situation. Becoming your own best friend and positive supporter will help you move past the pain to see the bigger lesson.

Understanding and growing from these lessons is how we advance mentally, spiritually, and emotionally, and that is the number one goal for humanity.

In this chapter, I want you to become an expert at identifying smaller situations and realizing that they, too, can cause us to suffer. It's like a tiny paper cut that never heals. As insignificant as the paper cut may seem, the pain felt from it can be intense. My goal is to get the reader to identify suffering in day-to-day situations and learn to make a conscious choice not to suffer. Learn to navigate each daily circumstance and choose the more positive option.

One day, my middle daughter and I were discussing renewing our passports for an upcoming cruise to Belize. I instructed her to call a passport company, get all the pricing and information, and make an appointment. While on the phone, I casually said, "Under normal circumstances, I wouldn't ask you to pay me back for this new passport, but since you lost the other one, then you need to pay me back." Instead of her remembering why I felt this way—acknowledging that she had demanded her passport from me a few years prior when she was living on her own in another state, and no sooner than I shipped it to her, she lost it—she got upset. She began to defend the fact that she was an adult and asked was I harboring resentment from her losing her passport.

I wasn't harboring resentment, but her negative, hostile response made me angry. It annoys me that young adults are so quick to claim adulthood, constantly reminding others that "they are grown," yet consistently making irresponsible decisions that parents have to fix. Although I truly enjoyed having her back home, the fact remained that She was twenty-two years old, living under my roof, and completely dependent on me for all the basic necessities of life. Yet in that moment she reiterated that "she was grown." It pissed me off, but fortunately, I was at work in my salon and stuck there for the next four hours. I had plenty of time to calm down. Even if the other person is dead wrong, we are still responsible for how we respond.

I believe God sent my daughter back home to me so I could continue to teach her the things I didn't get a chance to from ages seventeen to nineteen because she was out in the world being rebellious. Fortunately, her rebellious state didn't kill her, and circumstances aligned where I was willing to allow her to return to my home at age twenty. She encountered some harsh life lessons that made her humble and kind, which allowed us to bond deeply and we truly enjoy loving each other and living together this second time around. I definitely believe God orchestrated this entire situation. I was grateful to have her home, and for the most part, we had a loving time. I had changed, and so had she.

Because of our newfound positive communication skills, after this passport incident she FaceTime me about an hour after our little tiff and apologized. I was pleased, and all was forgiven. I have never been the type to hold on to anger until the next day. I train my children to lay ego aside and make things right. However, I do feel that in most cases, a conversation needs to be had. People can talk about what upsets them. Once it's discussed respectfully, we can all move forward in love.

It's imperative to stress that no matter how small the situation, if it causes you hurt feelings, stress, or pain, you are still suffering. One example was when I was purchasing new rims and tires for my 2011 CLS Mercedes-Benz. The factory AMG rims had been on the car since I purchased it and caused many problems. Due to the numerous potholes in Los Angeles, I was constantly getting the rims welded. It never dawned on me to simply replace the factory rims with more stable ones, which would make me feel more comfortable while driving. After using Uber for three weeks, I finally took the time to buy new stable rims and tires. I went to a place not far from my salon, within walking distance.

When I went to purchase the rims and tires, three employees were very accommodating and kind. They understood that this was not a woman's game, and I had no idea what I needed in terms of rim size and tire durability. They patiently helped me select the best options and even came to my home, which wasn't far, to change out one tire so I could drive to their shop the next morning to have the other three put on the car.

When I arrived the next morning, the manager, who had been the nicest of them all the day prior, was just opening the business. I wanted to leave the keys and walk down to my salon rather than wait for two hours for them to install the tires and rims. I walked into the employee area with a big "Good morning" and a huge smile. He was less than receptive. He wasn't rude; he just said, "Give me a minute." Now, there was nothing wrong with what he said, but somehow it still hurt my feelings. I assume this was because, the day prior, he was kind and attentive while I was purchasing the rims and tires. His dismissiveness the morning after was jarring, and it made me feel bad. (This is unnecessary suffering.) I left my keys with the other employee and walked the two blocks to my salon, hurt and annoyed. My mind tried to tell me things like, *Oh, now that they have my $,1973, they are not as nice.* I thought, *He is not getting this $60 tip I set aside for him.*

I am 100% sure he meant no harm, and I took it upon myself to walk my self-entitled, aggressive butt into a restricted area of the business. Yet, I still expected a happy, hearty greeting. This is my problem. He did nothing wrong. This is an example of how we cause ourselves pain for no reason. We make up stories in our heads and apply them as facts. Then we suffer because of it. Because I have done so much work on myself, I knew I was overreacting. By the time I reached my salon, I had concluded that this was just another moment of growth for me. I knew it was my issue, not his.

Sometimes unhealed people are like little puppies. We want others to pet us and lick our wounds. People have wounds of their own to heal. I allowed my feelings to be hurt. I walked two blocks in pain with a made-up story of my being rejected and dismissed by a man I didn't know. I did that! We create the drama in our minds. I am grateful that I have grown enough to identify these times. Even those small two blocks I walk in pain are too many. Any amount of suffering is still suffering and damaging to us as a whole. We can't always control the suffering inflicted upon us by others, but we have to check ourselves on the moments of suffering that we cause. These small moments are the ones I want you to recognize. Life will give us large undeniable moments to navigate through. We do not need to cause ourselves more discomfort with instances like this small one I just described. My nosy self had no business walking into the employee area. If I had annoyed him, he had every right to be. When we learn to transcend our ego and access every situation, we can take responsibility for the senseless suffering we cause ourselves. These are vital moments of growth. If we learn to tackle the small stuff we will develop the tools and the strength needed for the larger, more difficult ones.

My ultimate goal is to be the best person I can be and grow in all areas. I called back down to the Tire and Rims place and apologized to Edwin for walking into the employee area. He was gracious and I felt better, to the point of tears. This may seem like an insignificant situation that did not warrant all that emotion, but we must access and attend to all feelings. Edwin did not know he hurt my feelings. Nor did he know anything about my past maternal abandonment issues. That entire emotional journey with what was a stranger was all mine.

Throughout your life, there will be tiny moments that are designed for you to grow from. Seize those moments, reflect on them, and learn the lessons they offer. This is how we grow. The world cannot evolve until each person works on themselves and grows individually.

Here is some more "Daily Bread" for you to learn from. Today is February 13, 2024. I raised my children to always make others feel special. Holidays are a great way to spread even more love to the people in your life. People who say things like "It's just another day" or "I buy stuff all year long" truly annoy me. What is the harm in additional special days of love? They hurt no one. They invoke extra kindness and love. I raised my children to seize those additional moments to give gifts, hugs, and extra love on birthdays and holidays. Even when they were small and I had to give them the money to do it, it was okay because they were in training. It is a parent's responsibility to raise productive members of society who show kindness, compassion, and love to others. Teaching them to bring a smile to another person's face is a good thing. So, although I was rushing to get to work, I realized I had not bought my two youngest daughters anything for Valentine's Day. Since it was the day before the holiday, everything seemed to be marked up in price. I wanted to give them flowers. I spent $70 on what should have cost $30. I didn't have time to shop around and I didn't want to disappoint them. I bought beautiful roses for each of them and a card. In the end, the overpriced flowers were not as important as making sure each of them felt special.

So, as I walked in the door from work, I had a negative thought: *What if they forgot to get me something?* I dismissed the thought and came into my home office. My older daughter, Jayden, came in a few moments later while I was writing in their Valentine's Day cards. I tried to hide them with my arm because I wanted to surprise them, but she saw them. She left and came back five minutes later and said that she and Journey, my youngest daughter, were about to Uber to the store. Apparently, she had indeed forgotten to get me something for Valentine's Day!

This is the point of this story. I could have allowed myself to run with the *Oh, they forgot me* initial feelings that arose. My mind was saying things like *How could they forget me?* or *Am I not important to them?* Fortunately, I quickly cast those thoughts out. I knew better than to allow that thought pattern. I know my kids love me. They were twenty-two and eleven years old. I taught them well over the years, but this year they simply forgot. I could have chosen to be hurt, but I chose not to. They were young and still learning. As soon as they realized they had forgotten, they got up and went to the mall on their own to make it right.

Suffering is a choice. We do not have to suffer. In most cases we can decide to not listen to those negative voices in our head. There is absolutely no doubt that my babies love me and it isn't about the value of any gift. Everyone wants to feel loved and appreciated. Say the words. Buy the gifts. Make the phone calls. These are all additional opportunities to show more love and kindness to others. Why not? If not getting a card or making a phone call to your loved ones has even the slightest potential of causing them pain, then don't take that chance. You don't have to spend $70 on $30 flowers like I did. You would be surprised how even the smallest gesture can warm the hearts of those you love. A $2 card or a candle from The Dollar Store is just as valuable as a $500 dinner at the finest restaurant. Whether or not you give to others all year long, take advantage of those extra days as well. Don't assume people know how you feel. Show them, tell them. Take your mother to dinner for Mother's Day. Send your sister flowers for her birthday. Find out your coworkers' birthdays and buy them a surprise cup of coffee to celebrate them on that day. If people sometimes forget you, don't convince yourself of untrue and negative thoughts that they don't love or appreciate you. Learn to love and appreciate yourself so much that your inner love is enough, and everything else is just extra icing on the cake.

 Things happen daily that can cause us to suffer. Even the smallest of conversations can change our mood and lower our vibration if we allow it. Please don't let that happen. Not everyone in the world will be nice to you. Recognize these personalities and accept that you can't change them. Try hard not to take anything cruel personally and move forward. People who are hurting inside often hurt others intentionally. Send them love and light from a distance. You choose which thoughts to dwell on. If dwelling on hurtful ones causes you pain, dismiss them and replace them with positive thoughts. Let the "Daily Bread" you feed on be positive nourishment to the mind, body, and soul. Otherwise, don't consume it.

CHAPTER 3

How to Stay Positive Throughout the Disappointments in Life

By the second half of my life, I had learned many tools to keep myself uplifted and positive. I had read hundreds of self-help books and completely transformed my life from a depressed woman who felt let down by the abandonment of my mother into a confident mother, business owner, artist, author, and positive leader in my community.

I was born to two substance abusers. My mother had a vice for drugs, while my father had a vice for alcohol. My mother was cold, loveless, and abusive, but my father was not. He loved both my older sister and me dearly, often telling us he loved us, as he staggered drunkenly into our bedrooms at night to sit on our beds and attempt to give us fatherly knowledge. He always ended with professing his love for us—his two little girls and only children, who were being raised by his beloved mother, Ella Mae Fisher Fair from Dallas, Texas.

Perfectly Positive

He loved us without a doubt, but he loved alcohol more. My father died when I was ten years old of alcohol-related illnesses like cirrhosis of the liver. While he was in my life for a short time, he did an excellent job of expressing his love for his children: Mary Aurelia and SaBrina Romania Fisher. His name was Jessie Paul Fisher, born in Dallas, Texas on February 28, His mother Ella Mae Fisher Fair and stepfather McClendon Fair brought him and his siblings to California for a better life. I know little about his childhood, but as an adult, he struggled with alcoholism.

I believe having substance abusers as parents kept me from ever abusing any substance. I avoided drugs at all costs. In my forties and fifties, I would enjoy a glass of red wine periodically, but I knew hard alcohol was off limits. I had no desire to be disorientated or out of control. At that time I believed I had a genetic predisposition to addiction, so the overuse of substances was not an option for me. Plus, I saw the horrific impact it had on families like mine and many others. Genetic markers may exist in families, but I believe our minds and strong God-given will have more power. Bottom line: humans are more powerful than they give themselves credit for. You do not have to follow in the footsteps of others just because you share the same blood. You can be just as determined as I was not to succumb to negative addictive vices.

Learning to be positive is a gift we can give ourselves. It doesn't mean we are grinning from ear to ear daily and hopping around hugging random strangers and trees. It simply means learning to face each situation, assessing it—even if it is negative—and not allowing yourself to react in a way that causes you and others more pain and suffering. Look deeply into each moment and try to find the positive in it.

For example, imagine a young man showing up to work at a job he loves and has given his best to for over eight years. He is clearly next in line for the supervisor position, and today is the day it will be announced. He wears his best suit and tie, ready to accept his new position and get to work. During the meeting, the director calls a name that is not his. The director calls the name of a man who is hardworking and kind but, in the young man's opinion, not as qualified as he believes he is. He tries to keep his composure, but his heart is broken. He feels let down and overlooked.

These are the moments in life where circumstances seem negative. However, the young man's reaction does not have to be. He could scream, cry, and belittle the man that got the position. He could give a piece of his mind to the decision-makers. He could storm out, make a scene, and express his hurt and disappointment to all the employees. But that is not accessing the situation and finding the positive in it. That is not stopping, breathing, or thinking.

We can't always control the people around us, but we do have full control over our reactions to them. We can't control what happens in every situation because we cannot control other human beings. Maybe if the man who was passed over for the position took a moment to detach from the emotional sting of it all and truly looked at all sides, he might have concluded that he could have done more. Perhaps his ego convinced him that he was putting in more effort and dedication at his job than he truly was. That doesn't have to be the case, but we need to learn to humble ourselves and look at both sides.

It's also possible that he was indeed the most qualified and that the position simply was not given to him. Even in cases like that, we still must maintain control. We can't allow our minds to tell us lies such as, "You aren't good enough." Putting ourselves down is never the answer. We also can't begin to have negative feelings about another person. We are all phenomenal, and each of us has special talents and gifts. Although it is common to attack ourselves when we get rejected and disappointed in life, continuing this mindset is very dangerous. We are all great and need to develop daily practices to invoke that feeling of greatness inside of us in all situations. There is no shortage of blessings. There is an abundance of blessings for us all. We must learn how to vibrate at the same frequency as them.

Anger is a low-frequency emotion. Fear and self-doubt are also low frequencies. We can't allow our minds to wallow there. Even when we are hurt and disappointed, we must learn how to elevate our vibrations so that we can vibrate at the same frequency as the amazing blessings we desire in our life. Vibrating higher simply means, getting up and intentionally making yourself feel better. Use whatever tools work for you: get up and sing, laugh, dance, read, work out, pray, meditate, recite positive affirmations—whatever will lift your spirit. Do one or a combination of them all repeatedly. Eventually, it will become second nature and a regular part of your life, ensuring you live a better life than you would have otherwise.

As if staying positive itself wasn't already difficult. Imagine doing it when you have just been diagnosed with an illness. Picture yourself as a positive influencer, acclaimed for authoring the highly successful book titled *"Your Mind is Magic"*. However, you receive distressing news from your doctor: you have a tumor connected to your carotid artery. The surgical procedure to remove it presents two possible outcomes - it can either be a complete success, or a devastating failure resulting in permanent facial paralysis or immediate death due to excessive bleeding. How could one believe that staying positive is possible during times like these? Well, I'm here to convince you that it is. It's far from easy but possible. It requires daily commitment but it is indeed possible. Living in fear is not an option for me. I will enjoy life to the fullest no matter what. As I type this exact paragraph, I am on the Carnival Spirit Cruise ship enjoying a family vacation to Cozumel and Belize!

I have always worked out and maintained consistent exercise habits throughout my twenties, thirties, and forties.

Perfectly Positive

By the time I turned fifty on August 7, 2019, other than a few extra pounds and slightly higher than normal blood pressure, I felt I was in good shape. I went in for what was a standard tonsillectomy and adenoid removal surgery. There was also a small cyst in my ear that the doctor was going to remove as well. The tonsillectomy and adenoid surgery went perfectly.

However, when I woke up in recovery, Dr. McAlpin was standing at the foot of my bed, ready to inform me that when she entered through my ear to remove what she believed to be a small cyst, it bled profusely as soon as she made contact with it. She said she immediately realized it was not a cyst but a vascular tumor and informed me I would need another surgery.

Over the next few months, I saw a neurosurgeon to prepare for the additional surgery, which was more serious than the initial surgery by the ear, nose, and throat specialist. By this time in my life, I was mastering positive thinking so much so that I had written two self-help books: *My Spiritual Smile: Tools for Mental and Emotional Transformation* and *Your Mind is Magic: A Guide to Maintaining Positive Thinking*. Despite the wonderful new positive mindset habits I had formed, I still had to do a lot of work to not succumb to fear after hearing the news. It was not easy, but it allowed me time to practice the positive tools I so very much believe in.

These tools helped me tackle those days when I did an Internet search on my tumor. These Internet searches would always produce pictures of people with the sides of their heads shaved and deep surgical scars from the front to the back of their heads. I even joined a few Facebook groups for people who had this exact type of tumor, which at the time they believed was an Acoustic Neuroma. That decision was not a good idea. Being in the group kept me in a state of fear. Even once I had gotten to where I could resolve the feelings of fear, communicating with people who had unsuccessful surgeries and constantly seeing images of the aftermath and complications was not good for me. So, I left those groups alone.

By May 2023, after the COVID-19 pandemic canceled my scheduled surgery, I felt a twinge of pain in the area where the tumor was located. I created an affirmation for when I meditate. Each time I would feel the pain, instead of getting scared and worried, I would tell myself that the air I was breathing in was healing, restoring, and repairing every cell in my body. The air I was breathing out was releasing all toxins, sickness, and disease from my body. I convinced myself that the periodic pain was the tumor shrinking. This presents a challenge because it opposes logic. However, I strongly believe God has given us the power to heal our own bodies.

I was consistent with my "mindset magic" because I knew I had to reverse my way of thinking, but I knew it was possible. Mindset magic is the phrase I use to refer to the amazing mental power we all possess, a powerful unseen force we can manipulate for the good. Some call that unseen positive force God. Some may refer to it in other ways. Don't get caught up in the words. Just know that everyone has access to that power; they simply have to tap into it. This amazing energy is also in the words we speak.

I had to adjust my affirmation from: "I Am Healing, Restoring, and Repairing" to "I Am Healed, Restored, and Repaired." It's already done! We must believe and thank God not for what we wish and pray will happen, but we must sustain the unshakable belief that it has already happened. It's a mindset twist, but it works. Believe in the unseen, and it will appear.

Just because a doctor has given us a prognosis doesn't mean we have to fall into a mindset of death and despair. I attended all of my scheduled appointments and followed all the doctors' orders, as I would advise everyone to do. However, in addition to that, I used visualization techniques to imagine the tumor getting smaller and smaller whenever I listened to this particular sound. The sound I chose was 432 Hz frequency. I learned about binaural beats many years prior and would periodically listen to 528 or 432 Hz binaural tones or Tibetan flute. I find it extremely peaceful and calming, making it perfect for meditation. Since it was familiar to me, I set an intention that every time I heard the tone, my tumor would shrink.

This type of visualization takes consistent work and, most importantly, a strong belief system. The logical mind will attempt to talk us out of things that don't seem logical, but you must learn to bypass that and stay focused on the goal you are trying to achieve. Not every day will be a good day. On those days, it's especially important to implement the tools you're learning in this book. Some days, you may feel discouraged or have a hard time focusing. At times, it may feel silly, and you might think it's not working. Please do not give up. It takes repeatedly doing something for a while before it becomes a habit. Eventually, you will have practiced being positive so much that it will be a part of your authentic character. You are training your mind to look for the positive in all situations.

On January 1st and 2nd 2025. My tumor was successfully embolized and removed by Dr. Akera Ishiyama at UCLA Hospital in California. I was able to excitedly continue the second half of my life without the presence of that unhealthy invader but with the valuable lessons I learned from enduring that experience.

There was a time when one of my adult children went missing. They had not made contact for days, and we were all worried. Although this was definitely cause for concern, in a situation like this, you still cannot allow your mind to take you down a dark road. As the days went by, I began to have thoughts of my child being found dead. I even had visions of being at his funeral. This was a very difficult time for me, but I knew the dangers of allowing myself to be so consumed with fear that I tried to refrain from focusing on things that had not happened.

I understand that fear and worry can make you think this way—I get it. Negative thoughts will arise during crises like these, but you simply cannot allow them to linger. While my child was still missing, I consciously had to replace those negative images with positive ones. This is hard to do when you are overwhelmed with worry and concern, but I had to cast out the negative and replace it with the positive, or I would not have been able to get up in the morning. Three weeks later, we found my child alive. There were challenges they still needed to face, but they were alive to face them. Had I given into those images of death, I believe it might have been different.

If that situation wasn't debilitating enough, a few years later, another of my adult children went missing. Fortunately, by then, I was even more advanced in my positive thinking habits. After a few days of calling around and trying to piece things together, they were found in another state, though not in the best condition. As hard as that was to handle, I had to acknowledge the positive: they could have been dead. The phone call I received could have been to identify the body, but it wasn't, and for that, I was grateful.

Make no mistake, the conscious choice to stay positive in difficult situations doesn't always ease the pain or dismiss the reality of what's happening. In my case, it kept me from having a mental breakdown, which would have rendered me incapable of helping anyone. Pain is real, and certain life experiences can cause us tremendous suffering. However, if we train ourselves to stop for a moment, breathe, and think, we can manage it better. Focus on the thoughts you want to think about, not the uncontrollable ones fueled by fear. If you allow yourself that time, you're more likely to come up with the best solution for the problem. Those moments of silence and reflection can also help us accept the things we cannot change.

Although I know many parents have had to endure this disheartening experience, I do not believe God designed it for a parent to bury their child. Fortunately, despite some touch-and-go moments, as of 2024, all four of my beautiful children are alive and well, and I couldn't be more grateful.

We Are in Control

We must learn to control our emotions and reactions. No one can make you scream, holler, or lash out; you have full control over your behavior, even when someone provokes you and crosses a boundary. We live in a world with other human beings, and we cannot force our will onto them. Sometimes others are downright wrong in how they handle us, and we are justified in our hurt and anger. However, challenging or confronting them puts us in a negative headspace.

Sometimes, it is best to let it go—not only externally, but, most importantly, internally. Talking to yourself and having an imaginary conversation where you are telling the person off is just as damaging as actually confronting the person. Remember "What we think about, we bring about." If we hold on to anger, hostility, and resentment, we are the ones who suffer.

Internal peace is the desired result for us all. In some situations, addressing the person who has hurt, abused, or offended us is necessary and beneficial. However, it is vital to do this from a place of peace. Do not confront others while you are still angry or seeking vengeance. Some people have harmed us whom we may never see again, but we must release the pain associated with them and what they did to us. It is easier said than done, but it is crucial if we want to lead a happy, positive life and keep our minds free of negative thoughts.

Negativity will always exist in this world. There is nothing you can do to rid the world of negativity entirely. You cannot even appreciate the positive if you are unaware of the negative. This book helps you identify negative thoughts and replace them with positive ones. Darkness and light will always be factors in the world. Yin and Yang are realities of this world, no matter what. If only good existed, you would have no comparison. You can only identify good because you have seen and felt what bad is. You choose which area you want to operate in. Every day, you make a choice, even if you do not realize it. You are making a choice!

For example, one day, I had a tension headache, which is common. The week prior had been extremely busy, with long hours at my salon, plus a couple of women's seminars

I attended. I also took my kids to the Monster Jam at the SoFi Stadium, which kept us up long past my desired bedtime. When I got the tension headache, instead of simply attributing it to the long, hard week before, I started thinking it was because the tumor in my head was growing. This could not have been further from the truth. I figured since I felt the pain on the left side, near my eye and ear where the tumor was, it certainly must be a side effect of the tumor's growth. This is a dangerous way to think, but these are exactly the examples of negative thinking I want you to identify after reading this book. I want you to learn how to "Catch and Cast"—catch the negative thought as it comes in and cast it away. Replace it with a positive thought. I knew I had to cast those thoughts right out of my head, and I did. I took two Excedrin, went to bed, and felt wonderful the next day.

Identifying each time you slip into that dark-thinking place is the first step to winning the battle against negative thinking. When you notice the regularity of these negative thoughts, please do not feel defeated or disappointed in yourself. Instead, applaud the fact that you can now recognize and control when it is happening. If you do not notice the negative thoughts, you cannot change them into positive ones. Consider it growth that you can notice when your thought pattern has taken a turn for the worse. We can all lead predominantly positive lives, which will allow us to enjoy this beautiful life experience to the fullest. It all begins in our minds—master your thoughts, and you will master your life.

Perfectly Positive

Every day may present a circumstance that can upset you, but you can handle anything. One day, I took my middle daughter to the dentist. While waiting for her in the car, I used that time to get some writing done on this very book. I knew better than to let the radio play while the car was off, so I did not have the radio on. I waited for about an hour and a half, and when she was done, I attempted to start the car, but the ignition would not start.

The car's computer system had been telling me to replace the battery in my car key, for weeks, but I had not made time to do that because the dealership was far from my home, and I do not like driving distances. It was nearing 10:30 a.m., and I had to be at work at my salon by 1:00 p.m. I started to get annoyed. Then I remembered that all Mercedes-Benz cars come with free roadside assistance for life. I called them, and although it took them about an hour, they came out and started the car.

While waiting, I took a few deep breaths and pushed down the anxious feeling of annoyance when they tried to rise up. I crawled into the back seat and began writing this very paragraph. These are the daily life episodes where we must learn to remain positive. I filled my mind with all the positives in this situation. It could have been much closer to the time I needed to be at work, which would have made me late. It could have been nighttime instead of 10:00 a.m., which would have been frightening for my daughter and I to be stranded at night. I might not have been blessed with free roadside assistance and could have been stranded with my daughter without a plan. It could have been a much worse situation.

It may not always seem like it, but there is a positive in every situation. Sometimes small inconveniences, such as my car not starting up, force us to slow down and take care of important things we may be neglecting. I knew for over a month that the battery in my car key remote was very low. The funny thing is, I had no idea the computer in the car and the computer in the key needed to work together for the car to start. Mercedes Roadside Assistance came right out, started my vehicle, and then my daughter and I drove straight to the dealer, got the new car key batteries, and even picked up a couple of cute Mercedes caps while I was there. All things work out for the good.

I have been in many relationships that have led me to develop negative feelings. When you give your heart, mind, body, and soul to another person and they mistreat you, it can indeed put you in a very negative place. Staying in that dark place can cause you to react in ways that are not productive. Sometimes, we cannot believe the audacity of people who do cruel and disloyal things, especially when we feel we have been good to them. I know firsthand how painful these situations can be.

I have lost control many times when I felt betrayed by a lover, spouse, or even a family member. However, a negative,

Perfectly Positive

explosive reaction never produces a good result. While there may be momentary satisfaction, in the long run, you end up feeling worse about yourself for how you responded, which only causes you more pain and suffering. Your reaction does not change the other person's behavior, so it is pointless.

We have all been hurt by others. The emotions will pass, and eventually, the situation will not seem so dire. The pain will subside—trust me, it will. We must learn to remember that, even amid negativity, positive things still exist. Be patient with yourself, because all wombs will heal.

I was once one of those hurt people who lashed out when I was in pain. However, there is a better way. There is a way to handle pain and disappointment that will not make you feel horrible about yourself and will not cause another person the very pain you do not want to feel. When someone hurts your feelings, insults you or betrays your love and loyalty, stop and take a breath. Acknowledge how it made you feel. Give yourself time to process and allow those feelings to pass. They will, even though it may seem like they will last forever— they will not.

If you must address the situation, do so calmly and with a level head. Handle it in a way that does not inflict pain on another person. Returning to a place of love does not mean you have to continue engaging with the person or that you are still in love with them. It means you love yourself enough to react in a way that fosters love, not hate. You will always feel better in the end when you choose the positive over the negative. Hate, resentment, and anger can lead to sickness and disease in the body. Remember, positivity is not about perfection. It is about learning to stay positive even when life is not perfect, and that effort is worth it.

We can have a better world despite how horrible things may seem. Yes, hate, greed, crime, sickness, and death exist, along with a host of other horrific things. Yes, unnecessary wars are being fought all over the world, claiming the lives of many innocent people. However, even amid global catastrophes, you can still choose to focus on the positive. It does not make you a bad person to enjoy life while others are suffering from poverty and death. Those harsh realities will always exist, but we do not have to stay focused on them. The bad will always be there, but so will the good. Focus all your energy on the things that make you smile.

Dating

In my fifties, sometimes I would slow down and realize I wanted to be in a romantic relationship again. I had been legally married a few times, but those marriages happened when I was younger, and still dealing with issues that weren't conducive to sustaining a successful marriage. I did not know how to love or how to allow myself to be loved in a healthy way. As I got older and after doing extensive transformational work on myself, I knew I was finally ready to experience love again. I would beeline to an online dating site when that urge hit. Unfortunately, ninety percent of the people you meet online will completely waste your time. There will be no chemistry or connection of any kind. This is fine as long as you understand that it's a process, and meeting someone with the qualities you desire is possible. Online dating takes patience. Anyone who truly wants a suitable mate must make the time to meet in person, spend quality time, and get to know people. I was open to a first date. I believe that after that first date, both people knew if they had anything in common and if they wanted to proceed.

Once I became healthier mentally and emotionally, the dating process changed significantly for me. I understood the importance of not forming attachments too early. I don't mean being cold, distant, or acting like you don't care. I mean recognizing that this new person you've just met should have no control over how you feel about yourself. When we are learning to love ourselves, we can misconstrue something as simple as a person not returning a phone call as a rejection. That might not be the case—they could just be busy.

Sometimes, we create an entire story in our minds, telling ourselves, "Oh, I guess they don't like me" or "Maybe I'm not pretty or handsome enough." We tear ourselves apart with thoughts of unworthiness, even though none of it is true. Even if someone decides you are not the person they want to date, it takes nothing away from you. We should never diminish our value because of someone else's actions or feelings. They have the right to their feelings, and it's okay if you aren't the person they want to date—you still hold immense worth.

Both men and women can engage in this self-criticism; I believe that there is someone for everyone. We have all seen couples who don't seem to be a good match, usually based on physical appearance alone. But we do not know those people; we do not know what they see in each other, how kind and loving they may be, or what attracted them to one another. When we judge, it's often only based on looks.

I talk a lot in my books about dating, primarily because it seems to have a significant impact on how we feel about ourselves. Whether we are male or female, we all want to be loved. In the dating world, we encounter disappointments because someone we are dating lets us down or mistreats us. We internalize it, thinking there's something wrong with us. That simply is not true, and we do ourselves a grave injustice by allowing those thoughts into our minds. There are many reasons some romantic relationships do not work out, and there's no need to put yourself down or label yourself as the "problem."

For example, when I was in my fifties I began dating a man named Danny, whom I truly liked. Our first date was amazing, and we seemed to connect well. On the second date, we made the mistake of prematurely discussing religion—a sensitive topic that requires careful handling. Although we shared many similar beliefs, it turned out that he was a hardcore judgmental Christian who still believed that God hated gay people and felt justified in banning anyone who was homosexual from his life. I don't agree with those teachings; they seem outdated, man-made, and contrary to my beliefs.

Fortunately, I knew better than to get into a heated religious debate, so I changed the subject and I asked him if he thought our differing beliefs would be a problem if we continued to date. He said it would not be an issue, and we ended the evening on good terms.

One thing I liked about him was that he was always available to talk on the phone early in the morning. I love calling the man in my life bright and early before I begin my day, so the next day, I called at 6:00 a.m. We spoke briefly, but he seemed quick, short, and kind of rushed me off the phone.

Now, here's the point of this story: My mind immediately fabricated a story that went something like this: "He does like me anymore because we don't agree on religious concepts. He thinks I'm too strong-minded and is no longer interested." He never said anything of the sort, and I knew better than to make such assumptions. However, even when you practice positivity, life situations can still trigger negative thoughts.

I know that the mind can run wild with things that aren't even true if we allow it. These are the moments when we need to consciously reject negative thinking, especially when there is no basis for it. As the evening came, and I still had not heard from him, more negative thoughts crept in. I started telling myself terrible things like, "SaBrina, you are getting older; you don't look as good as you thought," or convincing myself that I had run him off because I talked too much—something I'd been told my entire life. I went to bed disappointed and sad, allowing myself to believe that maybe the dating ship had sailed for me and I would spend the rest of my life alone.

This is an example of unnecessary, unfounded mental torment. We must stop doing this to ourselves. Even if two people decide not to continue dating for whatever reason, we should never start attacking and belittling ourselves. Even when we make mistakes in dating, we are all learning, and those mistakes don't make you unworthy and unlovable. My point is that even though I know these positive practices very well, I am still capable of letting that negative thinking train take me down the wrong track. The difference now is that I know how to recognize when I'm on the wrong mental train and hop off and get on the right one.

The next morning, I got up and looked at my phone—no text from Danny. I told myself that it was good while it lasted and that I needed to figure out what I was doing wrong to run these men off. I accepted my fate and went on with my day. Then, about 3 hours into my morning, Danny texted me.

> *"Good morning, beautiful. Sorry about last night. I see you texted me. I was dead tired. I had a really long day at work, but I hope we can talk later. Have a beautiful day."*

Now, whether things worked out between me and Danny is not the point. The point is that we often mentally torture ourselves with stories we create in our heads, and that needs to stop. Dating is like fishing. There will be many fish we catch and want to throw right back into the ocean. Then there will be others that look, taste, and smell delicious but end up giving us indigestion and a severe stomachache. Finding the perfect mate is a process—make it fun. Don't let every failed relationship be a personal attack on your self-esteem. Enjoy meeting people, and if someone is not a fit, don't take it personally. Remind yourself that you are amazing and it's their loss. Never give up on the belief that you will reel in that perfect fish one day if that is your heart's desire.

I have been in many unfavorable relationships. So much so that in my fifties, I was a strict no-nonsense dater. On the first date, I asked every question a woman could think of to ask a man: Are you married? Are you living with a woman? Do you still live with your mother? Do you have a girlfriend? How many children do you have? Are you actively a part of their lives? Are you driving a woman's car? Is your divorce officially final? Are you currently employed? Are you an ex-convict? Are you drug free? Are you gay, straight, or other? Do you believe in a higher power? I was determined to avoid any of the pain and suffering that comes with dating the wrong man.

In August of 2023, I began dating a man who was well-known in the Los Angeles area for his funeral escort business. He was very nice and he sought me out on Facebook for many months. I finally noticed his persistence and responded in August 2023. We met right away, and I immediately asked him my list of questions. He told me he was one hundred percent single, that his wife had filed for divorce a few years ago, and then she suddenly recently died. I Googled him and found a divorce decree, which made me feel comfortable moving forward with dating him.

We dated openly, in public, and took pictures together every time we saw each other. We went to restaurants, snuggled close, and held hands openly. I had no reason whatsoever to doubt anything he said. Although I was a bit annoyed that he worked so much and had to cancel a date or two, everything else was good. He was attentive, complimentary, and generous.

One day while scrolling through his Facebook, I saw a woman he had tagged in a picture years earlier. Curious, I clicked to see if it was his sister, daughter, or perhaps the deceased wife. To my shock, she was his wife, and she was very much alive and well and still actively involved in a marriage with him. I was stunned. Who dates another woman in public, hangs out in restaurants, holds hands, and kisses in public when they are married?

At this point in my life, I was a successful business owner, best-selling author, and motivational speaker. I was a well-respected business owner in the Los Angeles community. He had no right to put me in that situation. I would have never chosen to share that type of time with a married man. Now I'm no fool; I know this is not rare. I just felt I asked enough questions for it to never happen to me, especially at this late stage in life with all of my over-fifty wisdom.

I'm sharing this story because disappointing situations like these cause us to question ourselves. They make us wonder what we are doing to manifest or attract these types of people into our lives. I definitely had to ask myself how it was possible that someone who had done so much mental, emotional, and spiritual work—and had fifty-four years of life experience—could again attract this type of man into my life.

I confronted Mr. Funeral Man, and he took no accountability for his lies. He gave me some sad apology but didn't seem sorry for his actions. His ego was so inflated that he actually began harassing me to the point where I had to file a police report against him. It was hard to stay positive in this situation. I was the one who had been deceived and lied to, yet he had the audacity to be upset with me. When I shared my experience with a mutual friend, it made him even angrier. He had someone, claiming to be a relative, contact me with threats, reminding me that they knew where I lived and worked and could get to me at any time. I wasn't afraid of him, but I filed the police report to be safe.

I guess I was supposed to just tuck my tail and go away, but I was pissed. When you are dating in your fifties, the last thing you expect to go through is this. One would think people would have gotten all of that out of their systems by that age. It was a ridiculously unnecessary situation, and I'm still mad about it.

I struggled to find the lesson I needed to learn from this, but at this stage in my life, I firmly believe that every situation, good or bad, has a lesson in it. These lessons will help us evolve into better people. It's hard for me to accept that when someone does something wrong, they can't just acknowledge it, apologize, and move forward. Maybe that is the lesson God has for me—to accept that I have no control over how other people respond to things. I can only control my own reactions and choose peace in a situation that could have gotten very ugly. As I type this, I'm not completely sure what the positive lesson was in this mess, but I'm determined to always seek out the lesson in every circumstance and grow from it. Unfortunately, we are only in charge of our own growth. We have absolutely no control over if and how quickly others grow.

There was a time in my early fifties where I dated a man named Jeff. I liked him for a brief period, We spoke on the phone five times a day, which is excessive but fun in the beginning. He was a fifty-five-year-old man who seemed nice on the surface—he smiled a lot and was quite attentive, which was a quality I definitely liked. However, his behavior was mildly erratic, and he made a big deal out of very small situations. I ignored the red flags because I was excited about dating someone I liked.

Perfectly Positive

One time, he scheduled a date for the following day at 4:00 p.m. The next day came and went, and he called me casually without mentioning the missed date at all. Initially, I was hesitant to bring it up because I had noticed his irrational responses in the past. However, I did not want him to think it was okay to continue this behavior, so I asked him what happened and why he didn't keep his word. As soon as I started asking about it, he raised his voice, got upset, and started screaming. That was it for me.

The younger, more insecure version of myself would have never dismissed this man so quickly because of an underlying fear of not being loved. However, by this time, I no longer had those unhealthy needs that would keep me attached to someone so unstable. I told him it was over and wished him the best, but Jeff didn't take it very well. He began texting me numerous insults, belittling me in many ways, and listing off the names of random women he claimed treated him better than I did. He turned into a completely different person. I clearly dodged a bullet on that one.

I felt proud to recognize my growth. I had long since surpassed the broken little girl who would have tolerated that toxic behavior and tried to fix this man. Love does not hurl insults. Love is not explosive. Love is soft and kind. We all deserve real love.

When I was younger, I developed a bad habit. If I was dating a man and could tell that the relationship was not going to work out, I would strike first. I would list all the reasons I no longer liked him and tell him it was over. At the time, I thought that was how you were supposed to handle such situations. However, as the years passed, and after a bit of therapy and self-transformation, I realized that I did this to protect myself from getting hurt.

A few more years and even more therapy and self-reflection later, I understood that it was not just about protecting myself—it was also about hurting him on the way out, punishing him for the relationship not working out. As I delved further into my own personal evolution, I fully recognized that this behavior was simply cruel. I would not want anyone to list all the reasons why they no longer liked me. Let me give you an example.

In early 2024, I was dating a tall, dark-skinned man from Los Angeles who coached basketball at a nearby high school. We went on several dates, and they were all pleasant. Although we didn't have the deep, stimulating conversations I love, he had a beautiful smile, was generous, and didn't mind driving and paying for dinner. He was affectionate, and we seemed to have great physical chemistry. He didn't pressure me for an intimate connection, but eventually, one evening after dinner, we went back to his apartment and had sex.

He lived in a tiny one-bedroom apartment with a big boxer dog. After approximately three minutes of intimacy, he fell fast asleep, leaving me awake to entertain the dog. The sex was horrible and quick, and for a few moments, it seemed like he had forgotten how to make love to a woman. He had been drinking quite a bit, which hadn't initially concerned me, until I remembered that he had to drive me home. He never woke up on his own, so after about an hour, I got up, dressed, and shook him fiercely until he finally came back to life. He got up, took another sip of alcohol, and found his keys to take me home.

I was beyond irritated that he was drinking more alcohol as we left, knowing he had to drive. I said, "Hey, hey, stop drinking, sir. You have to drive me home." He dismissed my concerns, and we got in the car. He drove recklessly and too fast, and when I complained, he drove even faster, laughing as if it were funny to scare me with his bad driving. Fortunately, I made it home safely.

The next day, he called, and I told him how irresponsible he had been. I didn't even mention the horrible three minutes of sex. The reason I held back initially was that I was truly trying to work on that lingering part of my personality that would express my feelings, even if it hurt someone. So, I didn't bring it up at all. We had a few more conversations where he boasted about our "great" sex. I was mortified.

I tried to give him a chance to redeem himself, so I came over once more. While he was in the kitchen, I asked him a simple, random question, and he snapped at me in a very rude way. When I came out of the bathroom he was standing near the stove. While walking towards him, I playfully asked, "Hey what are you cooking?" He snapped and said "Girl go sit your ass down and stop following me around my house." He instantly noticed my energy shift and ran over to apologize, but I was too stunned. I sat down for a minute; he apologized again, but I told him I wanted to leave. He walked me out in silence, and I could see he felt bad. However, the quick switch in his personality concerned me. It led me to believe that the person who just snapped at me was who he really was—possibly the nice man who liked to take me to dinner was an impostor.

Now I knew it was wrong to tell this man that he was a horrible lover, and I didn't say it in that cruel way. However, I did let him know how disappointed I was with his rude behavior and irresponsible drunk driving. I also told him that I was shocked he was satisfied with our sexual encounter because I certainly was not.

Now, I realize I could have left that out, and I struggled with myself because I could have easily just moved on without alluding to the fact that he was a horrible lover. I also know that if he had not snapped at me that evening, I might have never said anything.

The point of sharing this story with you is this: No matter who you are or how much work you have done to be a positive person, each day and in each circumstance, you still have to choose to stay positive. However, we are humans and still susceptible to the pressures of life. We don't always make the right choices, and sometimes we give into negative behaviors. I technically failed that time—I could have made a different choice. I could have kept all of that to myself. I was well aware that what I was saying could be hurtful, and I would not want someone to do that to me.

However, even if you don't agree, I still feel I grew in this situation because I acknowledged that I could have been kinder. I didn't say anything for two days because I had an internal battle with myself—and I lost the battle. Yes, he was a jerk for snapping at me, yes, he put my life in danger with his unsafe driving, and yes, he was the worst lover ever—but I could have communicated that to him in a kinder way, or not at all.

What I love about myself is that I am at a point in my life where I always check myself. I constantly acknowledge how I can be a better person. I do not always make the right choices, but I truly believe growth and change begin with acknowledgment. I am not saying I did some horrible thing to this man; I am simply saying I could have just left him alone and spared his feelings. I could have let the next woman deal with his ego. Yes, I lost the battle that time, but I am still very much a work in progress.

The ultimate goal for me is to avoid unleashing words or actions that don't come from a place of love. My goal is to be "Perfectly Positive" the next time around—to control the urge to say something unkind, even if it's based on truth. Just because something is true does not mean it needs to be spoken aloud. Or maybe I'll do some mental creative visualization and manifest the perfect mate so there won't be a next time.

I'm not perfect, and neither are you. The idea is to choose the kinder option when you find yourself in situations like these. The moral of that particular story is this: always stop, think, and try to come from a place of love, even if the other person did not give you the same consideration. We don't want to leave scars on people intentionally. Try to avoid causing anyone unnecessary pain. Fight the urge to speak your mind and tell people off, especially when you are angry or hurt. No good comes from it. Yes, there are important conversations that need to be had at times, but always enter those conversations calmly and compassionately.

If you make mistakes like I did in that situation, apologize quickly if the opportunity allows, and don't beat yourself up about it. You, too, deserve grace and love on this beautiful journey of life. Each day you awaken with air in your lungs, you have another opportunity to make things right. True growth is recognizing when you need to. I didn't always make the right choices, but I was determined to fully understand why I had the urge to cut the men's egos down as I exited the relationship. I knew that trait came from an unhealed place, and I'm still on a journey of healing.

Growth is a process, so be loving and patient with yourself, and never give up on becoming the best version of yourself. Returning to our true nature of love is the ultimate mission. I am so grateful to be on that amazing path, but it definitely comes with a moral meter. Take responsibility when you are wrong. Learn to treat others exactly how you want to be treated. On this path to positivity, you will learn to master transcending the ego. Yes, our feelings get hurt, and sometimes our behavior responds negatively to that hurt, but each time you choose kindness over cruelty, each time you choose love over hate, you are evolving. I wish that for us all.

What I love about mental, spiritual, and emotional advancement is that if each person monitors how they treat others, we can create a better world. By age 54, despite all the dating debacles I described in this book, I still wasn't ready to give up on finding a compatible mate. I wasn't sure how I felt about marriage, especially since, at this stage in my life, I had a home that would be paid off in two years, all my vehicles were fully paid for, and I had finally matured enough to resist the urge to run to the dealer for a new car and another car note. I had responsibly prepared for my children's future by creating my will and living trust, and I felt really good about that. I was open to marriage, but it wasn't at the top of my list. However, a long-term committed relationship was still something I desired.

After four months of casually dating men who seemed eligible, I met a man who had many of the qualities I loved in a partner. He was tall and held many positions of power—always a weakness for me. He was attentive and an excellent communicator. This time, I worked really hard not to let my old habits creep in. I didn't want to start picking away at him and sabotaging the relationship before it even officially began. He was a member of the same fraternal organization as me, but in a separate jurisdiction, which was perfect. It allowed us to stay private while we built a foundation and simply enjoyed each other for as long as possible. Life had taught me that was the best option. When too many people are involved in your relationship, it can be a recipe for disaster.

This segment is less about him in particular and more about how humans, who don't control their thoughts 24/7, can slip back into negative thinking patterns even after doing a lot of work to stay positive. I noticed early on in this relationship that this man wasn't as forthcoming with compliments as I liked. We exchanged a few pictures via text, and he didn't respond with the typical "You look pretty," or similar comments that I was used to. This led me to do something I don't even believe in: asking him if he found me attractive. Luckily, he quickly responded with, "You are a very attractive woman, and I'm very interested in you." That made me happy, but it also made me realize that I needed to assess why I craved constant validation from a man.

Yes, it feels wonderful to be told you're beautiful by someone you're dating, but those compliments shouldn't have the power to lower our self-esteem when we don't receive them. I ended the relationship once I realized he was simply too busy for a girlfriend. Each interaction has a lesson in it. From that short dating experience, I learned that my self-esteem wasn't as high as I thought. So, I went to work on building a stronger, more authentic self-esteem.

Perfectly Positive

In 2023, I essentially became a serial dater. I liked to exchange numbers quickly and meet up even quicker. I didn't want to waste time bonding with someone I wasn't sure I'd have any chemistry with. When I was in the mood to meet a man, I would prepare myself for the long, extended conversations that people usually have when getting to know each other. I would log onto one of the Internet dating websites and take it from there. But because I was always trying to fix myself and fully heal all past wounds and old toxic behaviors, I couldn't help but notice the universal need we all have to be applauded and complemented by others. It wasn't just me. One of the guys I dated would constantly ask questions like, "So, what do you think of me?" After our first kiss, he asked, "How was the kiss? Did you feel any spark?"

I'm never one to deny anyone a compliment, but some questions I would never ask because they reflect extreme insecurity. I learned two lessons from dealing with this particular person: no matter how intelligent or powerful a man may be, he still needs reassurance. Even if I got annoyed with him for draining me of every compliment he could, I had to realize that I, too, required the same validation. Maybe not as much, but I still wanted an acknowledgment of my value and beauty. Realizing this made me more compassionate and patient with his constant need for validation. I'm so proud of myself for reaching a point in my life where I can internalize things first. I look inside and see which behaviors actually mirror my own personality traits. Many things that annoy us in others are things we're also guilty of. I use that self-assessment to grow as a person. There is a fine line between enjoying accolades and compliments and crucially needing validation from others. Yes, it feels great to be told you're attractive, successful, and appreciated by others, but being able to do that for yourself feels even better.

I truly enjoyed filling this book with stories of how I found the positive in everyday situations. One day, I was meeting a guy I connected with on Plenty of Fish, an Internet dating website. This would be our first time seeing each other in person after a couple of brief telephone conversations. At this stage in my life, I was interested in dating and open to entering a long-term relationship. When I had time, I would meet a guy for breakfast, lunch, or dinner to see if we had any chemistry. On this particular day, I was meeting a guy at a popular breakfast restaurant, Roscoe's Chicken and Waffles. On my drive there, he called and said he had a funny story to tell me when I arrived. When I got there, I immediately walked over to the table where he was sitting. He stood up to greet me, and the first thing I noticed was that he was sweating profusely through his shirt.

I had brought a copy of one of my books because when he found out I was an author, he said he wanted to purchase a book from me. We sat down, and I took my book out of my purse, placed it on the table, and slid it in his direction. He glanced down at it, then smiled and began telling me the funny story he had mentioned earlier.

He started laughing and said, "You're not going to believe this."

I said, "What happened?"

He said that when he was leaving his home to meet me for breakfast, he thought he grabbed his wallet, but he didn't. I was not in the least bit amused. He went on to say, "If you pay for breakfast, I'll pay you back later today via Zelle or CashApp."

At that point, I realized I was being played and that he was attempting to scam me into paying for the meal.

I said, "Why didn't you simply call me and say you'd be a little late because you had to turn around and go back home to retrieve your wallet?"

He had no logical answer, so I stood up and said, "I see this is a game you play with women. You're way too old for this. I'm leaving."

He then said, "You're going to let this make you miss out on a good man?"

I laughed out loud, took my book off the table, and walked toward the front door.

He started following me. Every part of me wanted to turn around and tell all the waiters, waitresses, and security guard that he was a scam artist and not allow him back into the restaurant. However, I didn't want to make a scene, so I didn't say a word. I wanted to scream, "This fool just tried to play me for a meal."

I'm big on controlling my reactions, so I walked out of the restaurant in complete silence. He followed me out, saying something I couldn't comprehend because I had tuned him out. I walked to my car, got inside, and sat there for a minute or two. It's not easy to take the high road when you feel that someone is trying to take advantage of you. I took a few deep breaths, applauded myself for not acting foolishly in the restaurant, and suddenly realized I was still very hungry. Once I was sure he was gone, I got back out of my car and went back inside. I had decided to treat myself to breakfast. The waitress sat me at the same table where he and I had sat. As I was preparing to order, I caught the eye of a woman sitting at an adjacent table. She smiled and said, "I wasn't trying to be nosy, but I saw and heard what just happened with that guy." I smiled and went over to sit with her at her table.

We laughed and enjoyed breakfast together. When it was time to pay, I said, "I will gladly pay for your food before I allow someone to manipulate me with the lie of forgetting his wallet." She was very gracious. We traded more laughs and shared dating stories, talking about how difficult it was to date in our fifties. She turned out to be a really nice person, so we exchanged numbers and discussed cultivating a new friendship.

There is always something positive in every situation. Had I publicly humiliated the man and made a loud scene in the restaurant, I wouldn't have felt good about responding that way. In life, when we take the time to breathe, sit back, and assess a situation before reacting impulsively, it's always a better option. Rather than focus on the trickster of a man and the negativity of it all, I chose to honor myself and respond in a way I could be proud of. In the end, I met a wonderful person and built a lifelong friendship.

On May 30, 2024 my patience with dating was running very low. So low that after making contact with a guy named William E on Facebook dating I told him to meet me right now. I had no desire to waste time bonding with him for even one day if we were not compatible. Surprisingly he agreed and we met in Florence at a place I frequent called "Tals Cafe." He was tall and greeted me with a welcoming smile and a pleasant attitude. Breakfast was great. We bonded emotionally after sharing a few life stories. One being the death of his mother only a few weeks earlier. He understandably got emotional at breakfast and I was able to comfort him and share some heartbreaking losses of my own.

We quickly became an exclusive couple and things were great. He was attentive which I loved initially. He opened every door and paid every bill. We blended well together. He was welcoming and very generous with my children. He had a great sense of humor. As the months flew by some of his attentive behavior became annoying. Things like wiping my mouth after every meal and deciding when I was thirsty and putting a cup up to my mouth that I didn't ask for. People thought I had found the perfect man. He loved the camera and didn't mind performing with me and my daughter in our

Instagram and TikTok videos. He never said no to anything. He was open and verbal to everyone about his love for me. It was cute at first. We went on many outings together and had a lot of fun. Whatever I wanted to do or wherever I wanted to go, he was willing and ready. Eventually I realized he had no hobbies or passions of his own. No desires , no dreams or goals. No positive relationships with friends or family at all. He spoke negatively about both ex-wives and bragged about frequently severing relationships with friends and family, which bothered me terribly. I would try to introduce my positive outlook on life to him and he always seemed receptive but it wasn't who he was. He seemed to truly want to be a better person but found it easier to act the part rather than actually do the work needed to authentically become a better person.

 I enjoy being in a relationship but I also have grown to love myself so much that I equally enjoy spending time alone. He never tired of me. He always wanted my full attention which started to make me feel smothered. He taught me how to play pool and spades so I began having card parties at my home. We were in our fourth month of dating in September 2024. This particular card party was the largest I had so far. There were about twelve people there, four of which were children. At previous parties I told him he had been a little too aggressive with my friends and family during the card games. He had a real deep voice and a dominant demeanor. According to him he had forty years experience playing cards and he was the only expert in the room. That arrogant attitude began to annoy everyone in the room. I had been asking God why I didn't seem to have strong feelings for this man being that he seemed to possess many of the qualities I desired in a man. He was attentive ,affectionate, always available and extremely financially generous. However my heart just wasn't in it. We verbally told each other we loved each other but I truly hadn't gotten there yet. I know what love felt like and this was not it. I stayed because I was open to growing with him and hopeful of stronger feelings developing but they honestly never did. So by September I was already ready to end the relationship. He had begun having some physical health challenges that made him insecure as a man. That caused him to be even more clingy which I hated.

I do believe people come into our lives for a reason. I frequently asked God, "Why did this man come into my life and why can't I bring myself to fall in love with him.?"" There was something about the way he treated other people that bothered me. He was kind, loving and generous with me and my daughters but to everyone else in the world he was cruel and dismissive. It bothered me a lot and I thought it quite unusual that only my kids and I got to see a happy, loving man. If this is truly who he was then why were these personality traits only shared with us. No one in his family spoke highly of him nor he of them. I found that strange. It also became a concern of mine that he didn't seem to possess anything of his own. He had been in Texas for over 20 years and claimed to have moved back to California to take care of his mother during her last days. I often wondered what he was and what he had been doing all those years. Yes, he spent a lot of money on me but it was money he recently acquired from his mother's estate after she passed. I had the pleasure of sorting through her clothes and belongings to prepare her home, which he had inherited, to be sold. He planned on using the money from the sale of his mother's home and settling in California and building a life with me. His mother's name was Arthurlean. Yes, her fathers name was Arthur. While helping him clean out her home I bonded with her even though we never met. We were a lot alike. She was a hard working woman who retired from the L A Times after 30 years. She raised two children and purchased a nice home for them. She seemed to be a "make it happen by any means" type of woman like me. She loved cowboy style clothing just like me. I wore a pair of her cowboy boots to an event that he and I attended. I longed to have known her. There were so many similarities between his mother and I that I started to believe I was supposed to meet her son and indirectly connect with her even though she was not alive. I believed she would have loved me. William on the other hand, it seemed that he may have been broke and destitute at 61 had she not passed. All the money he used to wine and dine my children and I was money he gained access to after her passing.

I would casually ask him what his previous career was and what assets he had acquired for himself over the years but I didn't push for answers because I did not want to seem judgmental. Many women would not have been concerned since he was steadily spending money. However I was bothered and desired to know the true character of the man he was. Who was he before his mothers death? How was he supporting himself financially before he had access to her bank accounts. He didn't appear to be a hard working man that I could build a life with. I wasn't impressed by his generosity because I knew it was his mothers hard earned money and nothing he worked for himself.

So by September 19, 2024 the day of the final card party we gave at my home, after almost 5 months of dating. I was just about certain I was leaving the relationship soon. He made it easy by having an adult tantrum at the card party because I was not paying enough attention to him. He seemed oblivious to the many guests that were present and a witness to his childlike behavior. He stormed in and out of the house erratically. It made me and everyone in the room very nervous. I did my best to ignore his manic behavior but he kept asking to speak to me outside. The first time he asked I went outside to see what he wanted. He was angry and ranted about me not knowing the proper way to play cards. I calmly told him that if he could not refrain from being so aggressive then I no longer wanted him to teach me. He was furious. So mad that his lips began to quiver. He expressed an anger I had never seen in him before. I thought to myself "This is Over". I went back into the house to greet the new guest that had arrived and continued with the party. He had given me a cute card box that belonged to his mother. He decided to snatch the card box off the table in front of everyone and take it to his car. He exhibited unbelievable unstable behavior. I was done. I knew I would never see him after that day. I continued to play cards with my guest who kept asking me "Is everything okay". Finally he just could not control himself anymore and stood up mid card game and walked over to me and asked once again if I would come outside. I calmly replied "No". He then said "I'm leaving". I said "Okay, drive safely". Although I was very calm. I was very nervous. He is 6ft 1 and seemed totally out of control. This tapped right into my childhood triggers of witnessing my grandfather take the life of my grandmother. However I calmly refused to come outside with him. He angrily stormed out of the door. My fear made me hop up immediately to lock the door. Everyone in the room was stunned. I truly did not know what to do. The husband of one of my friends stood up and went outside to ensure he left. He attempted to come back into the house but my friend prevented him from doing so. He left and I never spoke to him again.

    I would rather be single than continue to date a man that has no control over his emotions. I knew that someone who was so cruel and spoke so badly about others' true colors would shine through eventually. I personally believe that is why I was not able to develop feelings. I could feel that ticking time bomb in him just waiting to explode. I left that relationship a little confused though. He seemed so nice and joyful initially. Although the attentiveness was excessive it seemed sincere. I had to go back and assess what love actually looked like after dating him. I realized that although I do enjoy a balanced amount of attention and affection. I don't need a man spoon feeding me and deciding when I am thirsty. There is a clear difference between love and obsessive behavior. I want a partner that has interests and hobbies of his own. I want them to have a life of their own that I can add to. I do not want to be their life. I learned a lot from the relationship. I learn to stay calm even when I am annoyed and afraid. I feel if I had not responded in the calm manner the day of the party that the situation could have been explosive. People come into our lives for a reason. This relationship taught me that all that glitters is not gold. I learned from dating him exactly what I do not want in a man.

Dating brings up emotions that broken people can't handle. Take your time and truly get to know the person. Try to ask the pertinent questions. Do not rush when getting to know someone. Inauthentic people can only keep up their farce for so long. If we all start to be honest with ourselves and others, we'll save ourselves and everyone else a lot of grief. In the end, the message I'm trying to convey is to enjoy your journey, keep learning, and stay optimistic.

We all deserve the best in life. We deserve a kind, loving companion. I love the idea of being in love, and when I date, I date with the intention of being open hearted yet wise. All connections will not be a match. Enjoy the process with no initial expectations. Loving yourself sincerely will generate a beautiful energy that will eventually draw that perfect mate to you.

CHAPTER 4

Be Intentional

We must learn to be intentional about the thoughts we have throughout the day. Even just a minimal amount of thought monitoring will show you how many negative fearful thoughts you actually have. Most of us are so busy moving quickly throughout our day that we don't even realize when we are focusing on fear and doubt and worrying about things that don't exist. Once we notice the thought patterns we are having only then can we learn to be intentional about positive thinking.

It may seem like a lot of work at first but trust me it will get easier. Start by monitoring your thoughts while driving. When we drive many of us are zoned out and operating off of second nature. We tend to allow a lot of worry into our mind when we are driving. Every day of our lives we must be intentional about positive thinking. It is not a battle you will always win. The objective is to make sure the positive thoughts outnumber the negative thoughts. If we put it in terms of percentage. Let your positive thoughts be 70% versus 30% negative. The important lesson is to be able to instantly identify the negative thoughts so that you can change them on the spot. Eventually your mind will automatically begin to reject the negative thinking pattern. As with anything you do repetitively, it will become a habit over time. I have been doing this work for so long that as soon as I wake up in the morning, before I open my eyes my mind automatically starts repeating positive affirmations. I used to record these affirmations on my cell phone and fall asleep listening to them. Now they are deeply ingrained in my subconscious mind. Find tools and daily practices that remind you to stay positive. A great number of what we perceive to be negative situations actually have a positive silver lining. We must be determined to find it.

In April of 2023 I joined the Inglewood Senior Center. I never would have thought to join since in 2023 I was only 53. However my daughter and I were driving by and she jokingly suggested it. The place looked so nice from the outside that I went down and found out you only had to be 50 to join. I was thrilled. I signed up for many of the classes they offer. One day I was taking a "Chair Exercise " Class for seniors and I walked in and there were already at least 20 people there, all of them looked to be 70 or older. I immediately began to think that they thought I looked too young to be there. This is how our mind works especially when it's filled by ego. This is another example of how we waste time with unnecessary negative thoughts. While I'm in the class, although I felt I looked too young to be there, no one asked me my age. So then I began to tell myself that "You look old, SaBrina. You are right where you belong. Clearly you don't look as young as you think. That's why no one even blinked when you walked in." Now this is an unnecessary pain we cause ourselves. Maybe I don't look old. Maybe they felt it would be rude to ask me my age. Who knows, but it does not have to be an assault on my self esteem. I don't have to let the voices in my head attack me. They are not always right. The voices are not always your friend. They lie to you. Be aware of these lies and reject them. We have got to be kinder to ourselves. Whichever reality is the truth, I still needed to be okay with it. If I am indeed showing signs of aging, I need to accept and be okay with that. Many human beings didn't make it to 53, but I did. I have friends who died in their thirties. By this time in my life I was determined to eliminate all suffering. That starts in the mind first. A lot of the pain we suffer from is in our own mind. The important point I want everyone reading this book to understand is that we create unnecessary drama, pain and suffering in our own mind. We tell ourselves many things that are not true. We can learn to stop doing that. I did not have to walk around wondering if I looked old enough to be at the senior center. I was old enough to be there. So I changed those thoughts into thoughts of gratitude. I absolutely loved the place. So it was up to me to create a peaceful, loving experience for myself there and that is exactly what I did. I set an intention to enjoy myself every time I walked into any room. I set an intention to accept and love myself even when I did actually see the visible signs of aging. If I felt insecure or self-conscious for getting and actually looking older. I changed those thoughts into thoughts of gratitude that I lived long enough to age. These are the little mind hacks we have to master in order to stay in a more positive state of mind.

No one in your life is going to be intentional about your peace and happiness. You have to do it yourself. You cannot depend on anyone to create an amazing life for you. Not even God. He gave you the tools to do it yourself. God gave you free will. The kingdom of heaven is within you. If you truly want to have all of the wonderful things life has to offer then do not put off learning how to get them for even one more day. It begins with learning to control your thoughts. Love, happiness, prosperity, good health and peace are all possible. All of these things must be seen in your mind first. You must believe that they are all possible. Perfecting the skill of positive thinking is the key to having everything you desire.

I set an intention for myself that I would not be an impulsive person. I told myself I would think before I reacted in all situations. I was not always disciplined enough to make that choice. I used to be an explosive person. When I was a young girl living in Compton after losing my father and grandmother I was mad, erratic and reactive. I never felt good about that behavior. However I didn't know that I could change it. When we are young we blame our behavior on a variety of things. We blame it on our zodiac sign or how we were raised etc. Although those things could possibly contribute to certain personality traits. Ultimately we have the ability to be who we choose to be. Free will and choice override all those other factors. No matter when we were born or what we have experienced in our lives it's up to us to determine who we are and how we want to show up in the world. If you don't want to be an angry person you must set an intention to not be that way. If you don't want to be a negative, pessimistic person only you can change that about yourself. I used to have a very bad temper. I would always describe myself as an angry black girl. That is precisely who I was until I set an intention to be different. I wanted to be calmer. I wanted to be a peaceful person. I learned that I had the power to transform any part of myself that wanted to change. I want every reader to know that they too have that choice. This is your life and you do not have to accept any description of yourself that you are not pleased with. Change is possible. You can be anyone you want to be but you must be intentional and consistent about shaping yourself into the person you desire to be.

    Every day there will be challenges. You have to decide how you are going to embark upon each challenge. That is why I wrote this book. To teach you how to manage daily ups and downs. It can be something as simple as a crowded store with long check out lines. It's your choice if you stand in that line annoyed and angry, continuously complaining all the way to the front of the line. You have a choice if you want to stand in the line or not. No one is forcing you to shop. If you choose to do so, decide to be peaceful about it. Spark up a pleasant conversation with the person in front or back of you. Use the time to breathe and people watch. Practice watching without judgment. Change your own negative energy and smile at everyone walking by. You decide if this is going to be a good experience or a bad one. You are in control of the energy you put out into the world.

Watching without judgment is by no means an easy thing to do. However it helps us remind ourselves that we are not better than anyone else. All people are different. Some are high spirited, some are more subdued. Some people speak loud and others are soft spoken. Some people are thin in stature and others are heavier. Human beings come in all different skin colors but we are all One. Our personality traits differ as much as our physical traits. Many people enjoy being around others and others are introverts. Some are loud while others are quiet. Watch and interact without judging them in your mind. We are all loved equally by the creator. It is mankind that creates separatism. Our ego causes us to internally judge others from head to toe. For example: Imagine you see someone in the parking lot through an office window in what appears to be a verbal argument with their spouse. You don't know either of these people so the egoic mind starts to create a story. Without any proof we label them both as being in a dysfunctional abusive relationship. The man grabs the arm of the woman and from that gesture we determine in our mind that he is the more aggressive one. All from what we see from the office window. None of what we made up in our mind could be true. They could have been discussing her treatment for cancer. Him grabbing her arm could have been a gesture to convince her to follow through with Chemo. The point is when the mind doesn't know, it will create a narrative. The story it makes up may not be a positive one. This is precisely how we embark upon everyday life. We make up untrue scenarios and convince ourselves that they are true. When it comes to others we label them and create stories of who we think they are. At times we use our own made up stories as an excuse to distance ourselves from them even when they haven't done anything to us. We become their judge and jury and we issue a sentence all from our fictitious thoughts. This harsh way in which we judge others is the same way we judge ourselves. We can be our own worst enemy. Observing ourselves and others without casting imaginary judgments is vitally important to our mental and emotional evolution. We do not have to believe every thought that runs through our mind. If it's a positive thought that makes us feel good about ourselves and others then we should keep it. If it is a negative thought that causes bad feelings towards other human beings and most importantly ourselves. Then cast it out of your mind quickly. It is truly just that simple. If it is God, It's God. If it makes you or someone else feel bad or causes mental, emotional stress or pain then toss it out.

As a salon owner for over 26 years I have definitely had clients that made it difficult to maintain a positive mindset while doing their hair. One in particular was this strong willed Nigerian man. On the surface he was kind but he had a huge aura of superiority and every time he came into my salon he would ask me to turn my television down giving no regard or care to the fact that I may have been watching it. His business meetings that he had while sitting in my chair always took precedence over everything else. Overall he was a nice man, very well spoken and polite but demanding and authoritative all in the same breath. It annoyed me greatly and made me not want to continue to do his hair. He tipped very well and because of that he thought it was okay to be late or change his appointment at the last minute. I finally got fed up and the last time he canceled an appointment and tried to reschedule for a day that was already booked by another client I told him nicely that we were done doing business. I told him that his continued tardiness caused me to have to work under stress because I would make myself late for the client that was booked behind him. He then responded by reminding me of the huge tips he gives me and suggesting that because of the additional money I should be available for him at the last minute. I told him all of my client tips well because I am excellent at what I do and if

I had to choose between him being on time or giving me a tip. He could keep the tip. I would no longer accept him arriving late to his appointment because it causes me stress and at that stage of my life I was not allowing anyone or anything to cause me stress. I wished him well and good luck in his pursuit for a new Dreadlock Stylist. He waited about three weeks and he texted and apologized and told me he understood and would not be late again. Reluctantly I agreed to take him back on as a client. I never had any more problems whatsoever out of this man and I'm no longer filled with tension when I do his hair. All things work out for the good.

Just when I felt like I had gained full control of my thoughts and emotions, something happened that would have been challenging for anyone to deal with. I was on the television show "The People's Court." One of my clients, who was a scammer, attempted to sue me for $9,000. She alleged that I did not have any mirrors inside my salon, claiming she was unable to view the progress of her hair. Not only did I have mirrors, but I also had a gigantic floor-to-ceiling mirror that she was photographed sitting next to. Once I presented my evidence, the judge immediately saw through her deception, and she lost the case without receiving a penny from her bogus lawsuit.

However, the plaintiff was so upset that her ridiculous scam didn't work that when the episode aired, she began a huge social media smear campaign against me. She started insulting me in every way possible, and unfortunately, because we live in a world where insults and negativity are more interesting than compliments and positivity, the Internet blew up. Many people joined the smear campaign and began insulting me as well. Popular YouTube vloggers shared a clip of me from "The People's Court" where they made fun of my forehead. Complete strangers were cruel and insensitive, picking apart every bit of my physical appearance. Someone even took small clips of the video of me exiting the courtroom and made more humiliating clips with me as the star.

It was not easy to deal with. I tried to utilize all the wonderful self-esteem tools I had taught myself over the years. I tried to ignore it, but so many of my friends and family kept sending me the horribly insulting video clips. I created a positive response video on my YouTube page called "Just One Day of Kindness," urging people to be kinder. I reminded people in my video that many are strong enough emotionally to handle cyber attacks like these, but most are not. Although I was one of the stronger ones because of all the work I had done on myself in previous years, it was still a huge blow to my self-esteem. Making the positive response video made me feel better. It made me feel like I was taking a really negative situation and turning it into a positive one.

The smart thing to do would have been not to read the comments. I tried, but I could not gather the strength to ignore them. Instead, I would go through each harsh comment and respond with something positive. I would match every insult with a compliment. I sincerely believe this is the only way the world can change. It wasn't the majority, but many people apologized and told me I made them think about how to treat others better. A lot of people secretly apologized because publicly apologizing on the same thread where they insulted me was "not cool," so they slid into my inbox and DMs to tell me how sorry they were. I was okay with that and felt it was a huge step for mankind. Many even removed their negative comments about me. I believe the world can change if we reach the hearts of mankind one person at a time.

The larger lesson was that I needed to learn that the more popular you become, the more eyes are on you, and you are exposed to the cruelty of the world. You cannot allow it to destroy you. We must build an authentic, impenetrable self-esteem. Many young people are taking their lives because of Internet attacks and cyberbullying, and this has to stop. No one deserves to be publicly ridiculed or humiliated. Now that we have social media, it makes hurting others easier for some and gives them the ability to hide behind a profile. We have to find our inner strength and confidence and teach our children how to develop theirs as well.

Although there were many days when I had to encourage myself while dealing with this, at some point it seemed to die down. Suddenly, someone would recirculate the video, and it would start all over again. It was painful, but I believe

God needed me to learn a lesson from this. The reason I believe it hurt so much was because it was partially true. I was indeed experiencing some hair loss around my hairline due to the high blood pressure medicine I was on. It was a fact that I had not even noticed. I had built up strong self-worth so that when I looked in the mirror, I saw nothing but perfection. This situation taught me that I had more work to do. I had to truly love myself despite any flaws the world would point out and learn not to take anyone's insults to heart. This situation made me realize that it was easier said than done.

I had, in fact, done a lot of self-worth work over the years, but this pushed me to do even more. I looked in the mirror often and said, "Maybe my forehead is big," or "Maybe my hairline is receding." I had to learn that even if these things were true, I still had to look in the mirror and love what I saw. I have always loved the way I look—a cute little brown-skinned, fat-cheeked black girl. I never questioned if I was attractive or not until this incident happened. I suffered through it and came out stronger in the end. I learned that all beauty will fade for everyone. Even the national beauty kings and queens of the world can't sustain the same level of beauty as they age, which is why the plastic surgery industry is so lucrative. I had to go back to the drawing board and truly develop unshakable self-love. That is the type of love I want everyone to have for themselves.

As horrific as that incident was, it gave me the opportunity to recognize a problem and fix it before it was too late. There were many ways to re-stimulate hair growth, but because I didn't realize it was thinning, I didn't do anything to regrow my hairline. Although I educated myself and addressed it quickly, I also stated to myself that I had to be okay even if it never grew back. Accepting this was very important to me. My worth was not in my hair. The body was never designed to last forever. It will break down with age, and we have to still see value in and love ourselves. There is a global lesson for mankind here. Internal love has to be a goal for us all to evolve. Beauty is like flowers. When someone brings you a beautiful bouquet of flowers, as gorgeous as they are, they will still die. Enjoy them just like our beautiful bodies. They are designed to return to the dust from which they came. Teach yourself to love the inner you so that when the outer you declines, it doesn't affect how you feel about yourself.

Enjoy your youth and beauty, but accept that age is a blessing, not a curse. Now when I see crow's feet or age spots, I change "I'm getting old" to "I'm so grateful to have lived long enough to see the second half of life." Welcome and embrace age, and do it gracefully. Life is a gift. Open it, enjoy it. It's a privilege to live a long life. But the ultimate gift is learning to love yourself as much internally as you do externally by the time you reach your wisdom years. Physical beauty is great, but finding the true beauty inside ourselves is absolutely priceless.

CHAPTER 5

Imagine the Best

In order to have the best you must think that way. You must think that "The Best" is possible and believe that you deserve it. The imagination is a great way to develop that mindset. The imagination is a magnificent tool. I consider the imagination a gift from God. We must see something in our mind long before it ever shows up in our lives. Learning to think positively allows us to sharpen our imagination. If you stop for a second and reflect, you will notice that many of the thoughts you focus on have also been creating a mental picture in our mind. You have been imagining it. Now this is great if the images you are using your imagination to create are good ones. If the things you are planting in our minds are wonderful things that bring you happiness and joy then you have nothing to worry about. You are headed down the right road. However once you actually take the time to dissect your thoughts you will notice that you imagine not only good things, but horrible things as well. We all spend a lot of time thinking about the things we do not want to happen in our lives. The things that we are afraid of also seep into our imagination as well. These are the thoughts we want to convert into positive ones. Instead of thinking you will never find love. Convert that into a beautiful thought, maybe an image of you and your new mate, madly in love on an amazing tropical vacation. Instead of believing your business will fail. Create a mental image of you at your business's 15 year anniversary party. Picture all your friends and family surrounding you, celebrating you and wishing you 15 more years in business.

I wrote this particular book to teach you how to cast out the negative thoughts and keep the positive thoughts as the predominant thoughts. You create your reality with the thoughts you hold in your mind. Don't be upset with yourself for having negative thoughts. On the contrary, be pleased with yourself for being able to recognize them. Only when you acknowledge their existence, can you change them. Having the thought is not the problem but allowing your mind to stay focused on the bad thought is. Having a fleeting negative thought is less of a concern than allowing your mind to stay focused on that thought. Think it, realize it is negative and then stop your mind in its tracks and replace that thought with a positive one. When I speak motivationally I teach the **"Recognize, Reject, Replace"** concept. It is also the title of Chapter nine in my second book "*Your Mind Is Magic.*" Recognizing negative thoughts is the first step. Making a conscious choice to reject those thoughts is the second step. Replacing the negative thoughts with positive ones is the final step. Master this concept and it will change your life.

We create bad imaginary situations in our head and actually suffer the emotions associated with them. For example, one day my two youngest daughters and I were driving down the street coming from shopping. My 10 year old said she needed to do her homework in Google Docs. Since I use Google Docs to create my books. I replied "Please make sure you create your own account because I don't need anything going wrong with my books." She is known for changing passwords and creating accounts she can't remember how to get back into. I began to get angry at the idea of her accidentally getting into my google docs account and deleting some of my work. The entire rest of the ride home I felt myself getting more and more mad. I had to remind myself that this situation did not happen. The simple idea of it had me livid. Which caused me unnecessary suffering at that moment. I literally had to internally say to myself "She didn't do it yet SaBrina, this didn't happen". This is that self check tool I speak of often in this book. Her simply mentioning Google Docs made me create that entire hypothetical situation in my mind and actually get mad about it. Which caused a physical reaction from my body, for something that never actually took place. Many of us do this from time to time. We invent drama in our own heads and mentally and physically react to it as if it is a reality. We imagine things and literally allow ourselves to generate the same emotions as if it actually happened. This is unnecessary mental anguish. This pointless suffering can be avoided. This is creating hell on earth in that moment for ourselves. Here I am riding home mad at my 10 year old for something that never happened. I believe if we don't stop negative thinking such as this in its tracks then we will manifest that exact imaginary situation. If we keep imagining something terrible happening, eventually it will. Self regulation is a key component in mastering positive thinking. We suffer through so many harmful, hurtful situations in our mind that may never actually happen. Let's save those emotions for real life circumstances.

Our imagination is a gift. Let's use that gift to enhance our lives, not cause ourselves more pain and strife. Life can be a wonderful experience once we eliminate unnecessary suffering. I know most humans believe that they have no control over what happens in their lives but this is simply untrue. The Divine Creator of us all, whom I choose to call God, gave us control over our lives. We were given free will. This allows us the ability to create. No we can't control everything but we can learn to control how we think and our thoughts are a vital key to the situations and circumstances that show up in our lives. Having a better life experience depends greatly upon the thoughts we choose to focus on. This book's purpose is to teach you the importance of controlling your thought patterns and making sure the predominant thoughts are positive.

Suffering is not always caused by us but in many instances we allow other people to cause us unnecessary pain. For example in September of 2023 I received the 2 Citation from the City of Los Angeles for parking my H2 Hummer on my grass. I have owned this property since 2000 and I simply don't drive the big tank anymore. I didn't want to sell it because I purchased it in 2003 when Hummers first came out at the full price of $85,000. Even though it was inoperable due to sitting on my front lawn for 6 years straight. I still was undecided about selling it. Many people had knocked on my front door over the years offering to buy it. I always said "Nope I'm gonna fix it up one day". Well that day never came and heading into the 7th year of it, sitting there with dry rotted tires and a kill switch that I didn't know how to turn back on, I still wasn't ready to sell it. Parting with it was not yet an option.

I began to get citations from the city of Los Angeles. After conversing with a neighbor who planted the idea in my head that another neighbor was the culprit who had actually called the city of Los Angeles to complain, I got mad. I didn't know which noisy neighbor made the phone call or if it was even true, but I accepted it as fact and developed an attitude about it. I scanned the street daily with my eyes shooting negative beams of bad energy to the neighbor or neighbors I felt were capable of causing me this unnecessary expense. Up until this point I had never had any problems with my neighbors for the entire 23 years I lived there. They were all much older than me and looked out for me like parents. The point to this is for however long I waged a mental and emotional war on the suspected neighbor only I was suffering. I was causing myself emotional distress. They had no idea I was mad and possibly not even one of them called the city. Maybe the City inspector was just driving by and stopped. He could have noticed the truck sitting on the grass with two flat tires himself. Maybe there is a law that says you can't park a car on your grass for 6 years. Who knows, but I caused myself to have an internal battle which provoked harsh feelings about others for no darn reason. I made a choice to suffer inside every time I got mad. Every time I screamed to myself "This is my property, they need to mind their own business." I was suffering inside and allowing negative feelings that did not serve me well. To this day not one of my neighbors knows about this all out war I waged on them because it all happened inside of me. I was fighting the battle from the north, south, east and west all on my own. If I saw one of them outside in their yard I waved and said "Good Morning as usual." They were none the wiser. I have to laugh at this because many of us do this. So many times we harbor ill feelings with misinformation. If we want peace internally we must learn to identify and stop this behavior. The thoughts we hold in our mind need to align with the desired outcome. We should take a moment and intentionally imagine the positive relationships we want to have with others. Imagine the ideal outcome of a challenging situation. For Example, I could take a few minutes, close my eyes and imagine receiving a letter from the City inspector saying that the fees for parking my truck on my grass have been waived. Remember "All Things Are Possible," so don't allow your logical mind to talk you out of things. Don't think about the bad that can happen. I understand that retraining your mind takes focus and a lot of conscious mental action but it will be beneficial in the long run. The imagination is a beautiful gift from the creator that allows us to create a life of love, peace, happiness, great health and abundance. If you can Imagine it you can have it. Try to commit to a few moments a day to sit alone quietly and purposefully imagine the life you desire. Imagine the best, not the worst. Imagine good not bad. Imagine happiness not sadness. Imagine wealth not poverty and do it so regularly that it becomes a habit. This is how we change our lives for the better.

Miracles

We say we believe in miracles. However when they actually happen the logical brain instantly tries to dismiss the fact that it is simply a miracle. One day in 2023 my daughters and I were driving down Slauson Ave in Los Angeles Ca and all the traffic lights were out. We came to an intersection that had become infamous due to a horrible accident which resulted in the death of six people there a year prior. The incident involved a traveling nurse named Nicole Linton. She was the driver of the vehicle that killed six people in the intersection in August of 2022. As I got closer to the intersection I began to feel a little anxiety due to the intersection's deathly history and because all lights were out. The traffic lights had failed from the north, south, east and west. Although most people know the rules of the road and to implement stop and go when lights are out. Some people simply don't adhere to that. I was beginning to get nervous. I was two cars away from being the next car to cross the intersection and I began to pray aloud. "Lord, please keep us covered and protected with your blood. Please make sure everyone makes it through the intersection safely." Mid prayer and right before I was next to cross the intersection. All the street lights miraculously popped back on. This happened while I was still praying before the street police had a chance to arrive to direct traffic safely. The lights just came on by themselves. Instantly it was my car's turn to cross the intersection. WOW! I looked at my daughter in disbelief. I said, "Oh My God." Once again we had been a witness to another miracle that very well could have saved lives. I started telling my kids about the power of prayer and how miracles are real. They have heard it all before but it is amazing to see small miracles happen in real time. I don't particularly like driving much anyway. I don't feel I'm very good at it and I experience a lot of anxiety when I drive. This is an area where I have to commit a lot of time to making sure I'm not driving around town with bad thoughts. Particularly thoughts of fear. I can not even for one minute allow myself to entertain continuous thoughts of getting hit by another car or dying in some horrible car accident. However this has been a challenge for me. I began to notice once I got into my early 50's I was consumed with my fear of driving. I had to drive for necessity of course but I did not enjoy it. I had two beautiful completely paid off luxury vehicles but still didn't want to drive. In regards to finding some positives in the Nicole Linton tragedy. I think that deathly catastrophe made many people drive safer. It's truly unfortunate that so many people died. One of which was an infant child. It truly rocked the city to its core. However if indeed it makes some speed demons slow down and consider others while driving then that is some positive drawn from it. Many lives may be saved just from people being more conscious while driving.

One day in April 2023 I was driving with my daughters to an appointment. I had recently been talking to them about when they become drivers even though the light turns green they should not speed right out. I told them to always pause for a moment and of course look both ways before proceeding into the intersection. I was telling them that quite often there is someone trying to speed through the light before it turns red so they should always pause even after the light is visibly green. On this particular day It was raining off and on. I made a left onto a street called El Segundo blvd. Shortly after turning we came to a red light. Once it turned green I did exactly what I taught my kids to do. I paused, I looked right and then left and proceeded to drive forward into the intersection. Suddenly on my left side I saw a car flying toward me at an unbelievable speed. It was traveling so fast that I could see the water from the wet street kicking up all around the tires of the car. I screamed, turned my head forward quickly and pressed the gas pedal with my right foot attempting to accelerate and avoid being crashed into by the speeding car. As soon as I pressed the gas to accelerate I instantly glanced up into the rear view mirror I saw a cloud of smoke. Somehow the car missed us. I believed then and still believe now that a miracle happened that day. I was able to clearly see the car on my driver's side meaning it was already that close to me. I don't believe any amount of acceleration could have caused us to avoid being hit. Even if the sudden gas pedal push advanced us a few inches it wouldn't have been enough to push past the length of my long 2011 CLS 550. At the very least the back of my car would have been hit. If anyones knows how long the body is of that particular make and model you will understand what I am saying. It still would caught the tall end of the car no matter how fast I tried to speed up. But it didn't. My 10 year old daughter Journey was in the back seat. We were not hit at all. It somehow completely missed us. The logical human me is saying "Impossible." The spiritual me is accepting the obvious miracle that saved me and my two daughters that day. Although the creator gave us free will and control over our own lives. It's clear to me now that there are times when God, the divine source intervenes. It's so difficult for the logical brain to accept that. I went over and over it in my head. There is no possible way our car was not hit that day other than the amazing grace and mercy of God. I will forever be grateful

CHAPTER 6

Mastering Detachment

I was super excited about this chapter. The process of learning how to master detachment transformed my entire life. When you struggle your entire life with love or the absence of love, you form many unhealthy attachments. These attachments can cause you great pain. Because of being abandoned by my biological mother, my need for love was greater than others. Even though my mother's choices were drug-induced and perhaps "She wasn't in her right mind," it didn't prevent me from growing up feeling unwanted and unloved.

Love is our true nature, and we shouldn't have to fight for it. We shouldn't have to live in constant fear of not being loved, and even when someone loves us, we shouldn't be afraid of losing their love.

This type of love is unhealthy. However, many people experience love in this unhealthy way. Until we do the emotional repairs on ourselves that are needed to learn to love without fear and teach ourselves how to have positive, healthy relationships, unfortunately, these are the relationships we will build with others. It may very well feel like love, but it is not. Love is kind. Love doesn't hurt.

Until we let go of the belief that we don't deserve to be loved, our relationships with our parents, siblings, children, and spouses will all suffer. Every human being deserves to be loved. It took many years for me to realize that the possessive way I loved my children was coming from a place of fear. We have a fear of losing them because our love for them is so strong that we cannot bear the thought of being without them. However, we are loving them while carrying the wounds from our past that have yet to be healed.

Once I began healing and truly began knowing that I was a valuable person, my love lost the desperate undertone. By the time my children were adults, I was so full of self-love and admiration that small things like regular phone calls and holiday visits were no longer vital necessities. I was no longer crippled if they didn't reach out and assure me of their love. I finally loved myself. Loving myself became my primary focus. I enjoyed being in my own company. If my kids were busy with their own lives and didn't check in as much as I would have liked, I wouldn't take it personally, and it didn't crush my soul like it once would have. I could detach from that unhealthy needy, can't live without them, type of behavior. It does not mean your love for them has diminished. It simply means your love for yourself takes precedence over everything. You realize you too are the prize. You are a worthy, valuable being that adds to the lives of others as much as they do to yours. Arriving at this point in my life felt wonderful. People who have taught us to put everyone else and their needs before our own have done us a disservice. We can't truly love others until we master loving ourselves.

Breaking attachments productively is done in peace and love. It doesn't mean you love people any less. It isn't a negative "I'm done with them" situation. It means you no longer need their attention and presence the way you need food, water, and air. Other people do not control your life and emotional stability. It means that when you and a loved one don't agree on something, you no longer worry about the relationship being damaged and never seeing them again. I used to be afraid to voice an opposing opinion to my family. When you have those fear-based attachments, you find yourself not truly being yourself for fear of losing them. You become very passive and in agreement with things you very well might not agree with. You are subconsciously afraid to stand up for yourself or oppose anything because you think they will not love you any more if you do. Although I lived that way for years, this is not a healthy way to love. I do not agree with explosive behavior of any kind, but there is always a kind, loving way to express your opinion or viewpoint on things. Your voice matters.

It took years for me to realize I was creating unhealthy attachments to friends, family, and lovers. They all feel like actual loving relationships until you truly know the difference. This is your world. If life is a play, you have the starring role. You should give no one the power to destroy your image of yourself. Let's say you run into a person who you don't even know who is downright cruel. This person says something mean to you like: "You're fat" or "You are ugly." It is challenging to comprehend how a person can be so cruel when we are embodiments of pure love.

In the world we inhabit, there are many people who are truly hurting within themselves. Unfortunately they will lash out at others. You could end up being the person they spew their evil onto that particular day. You must detach from their experience. It has nothing to do with you. You can't take anything they say about you to heart—their opinion of you is not a fact. How you feel about yourself is what matters. If we are honest with ourselves, we have all said something unkind to another person. I don't point that out to judge you but to show you that we can choose to be better. We can identify the behavior in ourselves and others. We cannot change others, but we can change ourselves. We've all felt and inflicted the pain of hurtful words. Only then can we learn the lessons needed to understand it's all a choice—a choice to be mean to another, it is a choice to speak harsh words out of your mouth. We choose how we allow others to treat us. It is also a choice to avoid letting someone else's mistreatment affect our spirit, no matter who—parents, siblings, employers, spouses. Do not allow anyone to mistreat you. Usually, when we allow this behavior, it is because we have not recognized our worth. Regardless of who you are, you are worthy and deserving of love, respect, and kindness.

Detachment comes in many forms. After twenty-six years, I changed the name of the salon I owned for twenty-six years. I had to detach from the name "Braids By SaBrina"—a name I advertised and worked hard to make a household name in the Los Angeles community. My staff and I drove the streets of Los Angeles in my burgundy H2 Hummer, flooding businesses, shopping centers, and parking lots with "Braids By SaBrina" flyers for many years.

The decision to change the name and no longer offer the service of braiding wasn't an easy one. However, at this time in my life, I was dealing with a medical scare and a few months earlier, I had been feeling the urge for change. I had given twenty-six years to the community, offering excellent service and giving jobs to over one thousand seven hundred women—and even a few men. I trained them all to be professional braiders and taught them how to advertise and sustain a business of their own.

There were many difficulties in being a consistent salon owner and governing over so many young people. It taught me to be a leader and showed me I could accomplish anything I set my mind to. I will be honest. I ruled with a stern "SaBrina's way or no way" motto. At five feet, two inches tall, I needed to establish authority or be run over by my many employees. I gave my all to that business, and I have no regrets. I will always be known as the famous "Braid Queen."

To create a life of good health and peace, I had to eliminate the stress caused by my employees—getting them to take pride in the business and dealing with challenging attitudes and disrespectful behavior. As the salon owner, I was held accountable for their tardiness and rude attitudes. I had to address any of their mistakes with the clients because, after all, the salon was named Braids By SaBrina. I was young and a full-time mother, raising kids and trying to develop the young women who worked for me into potential business owners. It wasn't easy.

By age fifty, after receiving a medical diagnosis that required me to eliminate stress from my life completely, I'd had enough. I sat in silence in the salon while it was empty, and I prayed. In the middle of that amazing stillness, "A New Vision Dreadlock Studio" came to me. There was no doubt, I knew that idea came from God. This was confirmation that it was time to move on from Braid By SaBrina. It was a new day, and it was time for a new vision.

I still had four braiders working for me, who were honestly more of a hassle than any help. I informed them that the salon would no longer be offering the service of braiding. I wished them well and sent them off to implement all that I had taught them about building their businesses. Some of them had been pure thorns in my side.

I called the graphic designer and seven days later, all the signs, flyers, and business cards had been changed to "A New Vision Dreadlock Studio." The braiders worked on a sixty percent commission for every head they braided. With the new business, I restructured my prices for Dreadlock Extensions and Repairs. I started requiring deposits to get on my schedule. I never missed one dime and began making more money than I had ever made in my life.

Detachment can be incredibly beneficial at certain points in life. Braids By SaBrina served its purpose well, providing financial support for my four children. Now at fifty years old, I was experiencing a mental, emotional, and spiritual transition in my life, so I was ready for change. Not having staff to concern myself with allowed me to create a much more peaceful environment for my salon, which gave me a beautiful serene place to relax and heal. I created a meditation area so I could relax and meditate between clients. I loaded the salon up with beautiful raw amethyst healing crystals. I remodeled my classroom and began teaching dreadlock maintenance and beginning and advanced braiding classes. It was indeed a new day, and I had created a new vision for myself in business. It was the best decision I ever made. If I could not peacefully detach from the name "Braids By SaBrina," it would never have happened.

Ego can cause us to form attachments we know we need to release. No one wants to feel rejected or unwanted. Many people remain in relationships they know aren't leading anywhere simply because their ego will not allow them to end it. You can detach from others peacefully. My biological mother abandoned her six children. We were all dispersed in various homes and some were in foster care, preventing us from growing up together and forming relationships as children. Each of us had our way of resolving our feelings of abandonment. I became successful and the absolute best parent I could be. A few of my sisters have always treated me as if their lack of success was my fault. They would ask to live with me or expect me to assume responsibility for them financially. I came from the same mother, and thus I grew up being deficient in the mother's love department, too. When I realized that their intentions were not to love me and nurture a positive sisterly bond, but to establish a dynamic focused on "What can you do for me?" I was deeply hurt and chose to detach myself.

Despite being blood relatives, I was unwilling to let them make me feel indebted to them. After all, I didn't give birth to them. I was going through my struggles and healing process, just like they were. I yearned for love and had to seek it out, just like they did. On top of that, I had the responsibility of providing for myself and my children. Initially, I reached out to all of them, attempting to build closer relationships based on the shared bloodline. However, each sibling had a unique personality and perspective on life, making it challenging to form the close bonds I desired. I had to detach from the belief that family members are automatically close and come to terms with the fact that everyone has their journey, which may not involve you.

Each child had suffered different consequences because of our mother's addiction and abuse, leading them to develop habits that made it nearly impossible for us to form the close family relationship I desired. By 2022, I had not developed strong relationships with my siblings, including the oldest one with whom I was raised. Surprisingly, I was okay with this. I seemed to be the only sibling who wanted to bring everyone together and foster a genuine bond. My oldest sister didn't have a close connection with the younger siblings and showed no interest in forming one. Our relationship had also grown distant. We exchanged pleasantries during holidays and occasionally shared a photo or two, but that was the extent of our interaction.

Fortunately, I had learned to master the art of positive detachment. Even though my oldest sister and I were not very close by 2023, we had been raised together and shared the same parents. Regrettably, our communication had dwindled to just the occasional interaction during the holidays. Mary seemed to harbor a resentment toward me, treating me as if I had personally wronged her. This resentment seemed to stem from my early years of healing after witnessing the tragic murder of our grandmother, a topic I discuss in Chapter 9, and the subsequent abandonment of our mother and all the associated difficulties.

In the years when I struggled emotionally, I leaned on my older sister, Mary, for support. However, these difficult times caused her to become annoyed with me later on. This emotional dependence stemmed from the traumatic murder of our grandmother, who raised us from a young age. Witnessing her death at seventeen years old triggered post-traumatic stress and other mental issues that took me years to overcome. Our grandmother was the only person in my life who truly loved me, as our father had passed away when we were ten and eleven, and our biological mother was an active drug addict. These circumstances made me more reliant on Mary, who took on a maternal role despite us being only eleven months apart in age. While I had financial independence and shelter, I was emotionally shattered. Sadly, I did not receive any counseling or support to help me cope with the loss of my grandmother.

Someone who was supposed to love her murdered the one person who truly loved and understood me—especially when my mother couldn't—all right before my eyes. This tragedy completely shattered my world. I fell into a deep depression and struggled with suicidal thoughts. It felt like God had abandoned me, just like my mother did.

My sister Mary and I often disagreed because we both had strong and unique personalities. However, after experiencing such trauma, I felt she was the only person I had left. I didn't know how to make decisions or stand up for myself. In my eyes, her opinion was law and she could do no wrong. I had lost all faith in myself and became extremely insecure.

I was always respectful and well-behaved towards my sister. It wasn't in my nature to be unruly or disrespectful. Our grandmother, who raised us with traditional values and principles, instilled in us a sense of respect and decency. However, I constantly harbored a fear that if I stood up for myself, my sister would also abandon me. As I gradually started to heal from the trauma, I apologized to her multiple times for the emotional burden I had unintentionally placed on her. But she never treated me the same way again.

I grew into a successful, self-sufficient woman, becoming a business owner, homeowner, and parent. However, my sister continued to treat me as if I were her emotionally broken little sister who needed therapy due to witnessing the tragedy. Granted, I suffered for many years, struggling to find a way to heal from such a traumatic experience. As I got older, I took charge of my healing process. I let go of the victim mentality and stopped seeking her approval and validation for my adult decisions. I began to recognize that I was just as intelligent and capable as she was.

However, my sister never treated me as her equal. Despite her vows of love, she kept me at a distance. When I would reach out to her, she rarely took the time to respond, unless it was a holiday or birthday greeting. By this point in my life, I understood that this wasn't my issue to fix. It wasn't my place to bring attention to the issues I believed she had. I had done the best I could. I raised four children alone and successfully created several businesses that provided for me and my kids. I even bought a home a few years after she did. In 2023, my salon celebrated twenty-seven years of consistent business. In the midst of all this, I sought out Christian counseling, spiritual counseling, and every other form of therapy I thought would help me heal. I read and wrote several self-help books and took full control of my healing.

It took years to stop dreaming of my granny's murder and to develop authentic self-esteem. The mere knowledge that my mother didn't want me made it even harder to see my worth, but eventually, I overcame it. I successfully built strong, authentic self-esteem.

By age fifty-four, I was happy and content. I had almost paid off my home in full and left it in a living trust to my youngest daughters. My famous Los Angeles braid shop—Braids By SaBrina—had transitioned into "A New Vision Dreadlock Studio," where I finally enjoyed a peaceful environment that allowed me to only work four days a week, teach my braiding and loc extensions classes, and display and sell my art to clients who came to get their hair done. Life was great.

I learned to positively master the detachment that I stress to you in this chapter. I humbly knew I was the prize, and therefore my sister's distance no longer hurt me. I told myself that her not allowing me into her life was her loss and her problem. I am a great, loving person who knows her worth. I was not a broken little sister, crippled by the tragedies of my past. I bring positivity to anyone's life, but I reached a point where I no longer wanted to persuade her or anyone else about this. I don't have to prove my worth to anyone.

Her behavior would have crushed the broken younger me, who would have needed her approval and love as badly as I needed air and food. I no longer depended on her for my emotional stability. I loved myself wholeheartedly. More importantly, I no longer tried to figure out why she treated me that way. It simply didn't matter anymore, and I wasn't angry or hurt about it. She always verbally expressed her love—I will give her that—but it came with ridicule and reprimanding that made me feel like an ignorant child who couldn't do right. I won't accept that type of love from her or anyone else.

I had finally detached myself from needing anyone's validation and approval. I had finally found peace within myself and had accepted the tragic event that had haunted me for so long. I could identify how the murder of my grandmother affected my life and recognize the decisions I made that stemmed solely from the pain of enduring something so horrific. I was receptive and cordial when my sister and I communicated, but I didn't need more. The days of her inviting me out to her home and spending time together were long gone. I was okay with that. I was at peace and no longer needed anyone to tell me I was valuable.

I loved myself, and no longer put others before me. Whatever she was going through that made her distant was just fine with me. It no longer caused me pain. I now had myself on that pedestal that I once had her on. I realized I was just as valuable and worthy of love and respect as everyone else in the world. Most importantly, I wasn't upset with her and understood she loved her little sister the best way she knew how. She meant me no harm. These were the only tools she had. God sent us all here to earth to learn and grow. Remember: Breaking attachments to people never has to be done in anger. We can do it in love. By loving myself enough, I gave myself the best gift of no longer allowing anyone to make me feel broken.

Sometimes the ones who claim to love us the most can be the very ones preventing us from evolving into the great people God intended us to be. We are all one; love them anyway. Yes, I would love to have a better, more balanced relationship with my sister. However, if it comes at the cost of diminishing my self-worth and value, I am better off without it. Self-love is so priceless. Even on days when I wake up from a bad dream or some life experience that sparks residual feelings of my past, I understand them for what they are. I allow those negative feelings to pass. I do not allow them to make me feel worthless or to cause me to backtrack emotionally and undo all the work that I have done.

The journey to self-love and inner healing is just that. Each person has their own journey, and along the way, they may hurt others. I now believe that we are in each other's lives to help and assist each person, to help them resolve past karma and possibly work on personality traits that don't serve them well. We grow from all relationships, good or bad. In the end, the goal is for all people to return to love, starting first with themselves and then allowing that beautiful love to radiate out to others.

In 2023, my younger sister, Kaylen, had a heart attack at forty-four years old. She and I were still not super close, but I loved her dearly and she had been a part of my life since she was a very little girl. I am ten years older than her. She has very slight developmental issues because of my mother's drug addiction, but she is extremely high-functioning. I visited her in the hospital a few times before and after her open-heart surgery, and I was grateful that I was able to go. At this stage in my life, I was still working quite a bit in my salon, as well.

My biological mother had five daughters and one son, all raised separately except for my older sister and me. One of the middle sisters, named Verdell, who I don't have a relationship with at all because she is disrespectful and toxic, attempted to reach out to me during the time my sister Kaylen was in the hospital. I assume she felt that our younger sister's crisis would mend the rift between her and me. Now, this is where the peaceful detachment comes in. I wish her the absolute best in life. However, I do not want to rekindle a sisterly relationship with someone who crosses lines.

I have never been the type of person who would curse you out and cross all boundaries on Monday and expect you to love me and forget about it on Friday. Even if we are related, I refuse to let people like that into my space. Society teaches us that we must maintain relationships with family members no matter what. We do not, especially if maintaining that relationship interrupts your peace of mind. When I was younger and still wallowing in my self-hate and dysfunction, I kept people around me just because I didn't want to be alone.

After healing from a lot of my past trauma and growing to love myself, I began craving time to myself. I fell in love with the peaceful life I had created for myself. I fell madly in love with myself. So, although my younger sister would often ask if me and the other sister had made up, I had no desire to re-enter that sisterhood. Nope, and I was not mad, resentful, or hurt about it. I didn't hate her. I did not speak ill of Verdell, nor did I have any hard feelings. I simply knew that she could not be a part of my life, and I was okay with that. I call that a peaceful detachment.

I didn't have any negative thoughts about her, and I wish her and her children great success and love. However, I won't be allowing them back into my life.. Some may think that is mean and may find that difficult to understand. However, by age fifty-four, I had created a stable life of peace and harmony, which had no room for bickering or explosive, irrational behavior. People who act like this are what I call low-vibrational beings. I used to be one. I don't mean to sound cruel or dismissive, and I am in no way better than another human being. I prefer to always remain cordial and respectful, even if we disagree.

When I was younger and still operating through the holes of past trauma, I could match that negative energy. I could scream, holler, and throw insults right along with the best of them, but I evolved past that behavior. I will never be that type of reactive, impulsive person again, and I will not allow others to treat me that way. We must choose the life we desire. We can choose who and what we allow in our daily lives. If a person brings constant confrontation and a continuous cantankerous spirit, then it serves us best to love them from a distance.

Mastering this type of detachment has changed my life for the better. As a healed person, I now have the luxury of deciding who I share my life with. I deserve to be loved for who I am, not for what I can offer. I deserve to be given the same consideration that I give others. My toxic days are over. Thank God, I survived them. Now I don't accept mistreatment or disrespect from anyone. You won't be able to repeat abusive bad behavior and continue to apologize to me. Yes, we must forgive, but we do not have to allow that person back into our lives. That's a harsh reality for others to accept, but you must put yourself first.

You don't have to allow others to dishonor or abuse you. You can detach, wish them well, and love them from afar, without any hate or animosity in your heart. Anyone who does not bring love, respect, and peace into your life does not deserve to be there. The objective of this chapter is to emphasize the significance of cultivating positive relationships that enrich our lives. The title "Mastering Detachment" is about lovingly detaching ourselves from people, places, and things that cause us mental and emotional distress. Dispelling the subconscious belief that we must allow people who share our blood to harass and hurt us.

Granted, there is no life without relationships. They begin the minute you exist in the womb of your mother. You are instantly in a relationship with other human beings. You are a son, daughter, sister or brother. Yet the most important relationship you will ever have is the one you build with yourself—your most trusted ally. You will have to teach others how to treat you. This self-love, self-care, and self-preservation journey that I constantly speak about is the beginning of the new life you desire and the end of the dysfunctional one you must bury. We must never think for one moment that we cannot have the life we want.

After so many years of trauma, loss, and insecurities, it can seem impossible to think otherwise. However, I stand firm on what I say: it is your God-given birthright to live in peace, harmony, and true self-love. The only way to reach this new level of mental and emotional freedom is to have the courage to detach from people, places, and things that don't serve you well. I cannot stress enough that when we reach this new mental and emotional state of detachment, hate will never motivate it. True inner healing requires love and forgiveness for ourselves and others. It has taken me over forty years to reach this new level of inner peace, but thank God I made it.

So, as I teach you the concept of mastering detachment in this chapter, please understand that it is vital for your inner peace and happiness. Detaching from negative people is not an act of hate. Yes, you can still love those you choose to detach from. You can still pray for their well-being, safety, and happiness. Yet, you don't have to take part in their lives or allow them to take part in yours if they don't bring peace, love, and happiness. The key to mastering detachment is knowing your worth and refusing to allow others to make you feel inferior or worthless. We must break free from those who seek to harm or diminish our light, no matter who they are.

CHAPTER 7

Live For Yourself

I have four amazing children—one son and three daughters—and I absolutely adore them. One key component I learned in maintaining positivity is putting myself first. Yes, I know most parents spend their entire lives putting their kids first. That is what we are taught to do. However, if you do not put yourself first; you are in no mental and emotional condition to give your children the best version of you.

When I was a younger parent, I thought my feelings and needs did not matter as long as the kids were happy. Most parents think this way. They believe they must sacrifice everything because they choose to be parents. That was definitely how I felt. Now I feel differently. There is so much work that needs to be done to live a happy, peaceful life. If you neglect yourself and only focus on making your children happy, you will look up and find yourself a senior citizen who is sad, depressed, and unfulfilled. Your children will have married and gone on with their own lives, checking in with you only on holidays, busy creating their world. Making sure your own emotional and mental needs are covered first is not selfish. Life goes on after parenthood. I now know how important it is to make sure I am happy as well.

Because of my past, I have grown up with many emotional deficiencies. I felt unwanted, and my self-esteem was very low. I became a parent long before I even attempted to seek healing from my past. Because I still carried so much past trauma, my love for my kids was what I considered unhealthy. I was a great parent by society's standards. I worked hard and provided everything they wanted and needed. I even tried to make sure I showed plenty of affection and attended to the best I knew how to all of their emotional needs. I encouraged and uplifted them, hugged and kissed them regularly, etc. I went to all their school functions and always showed up for them as a mother. As far as I was concerned, I was the best parent ever.

However, that didn't leave any time for me to attend to my own needs. Honestly, I can't say that in my early twenties and thirties, I even realized I had unattended emotional and mental needs. Although I knew I had been through trauma, I didn't know I could seek help from the recurring memories and pain. I didn't know many of my fears and reactions to certain situations were direct results of the trauma I had experienced. I didn't realize the obsessive way in which I loved my children was rooted in fear and trauma.

Make no mistake, there are times when the behavior of your kids can be challenging, but when you are a healed person, you can respond differently. When you are broken and needy, the kids can do no wrong. Once you work on yourself, you realize you are just as valuable as they are, and you deserve the same type of love and respect that you give to them. Once you heal, you establish healthy boundaries for yourself and refuse to let anyone, including the little people you gave birth to, mistreat you. When you heal from your emotional wounds, you learn to respond to situations differently. Everyone is not the enemy. Everyone is not trying to hurt or offend you. Hurt people live with a fear of enduring more hurt and are always on guard.

    I remember a time when my older sister, who had been away at college, said she was not going to be coming home for Thanksgiving. It seems normal for a new, adjusting college student when I look at it now, but back then, my reaction was one of hurt and devastation. I cried and took it personally that she wasn't coming home for the holiday. Her decision had nothing to do with me. She was new to college life and had a new job to juggle. But because of my unhealed abandonment issues from our mother, I interpreted her not coming home as her not viewing me as important enough to come home to see. That wasn't the case at all, but because I never sought healing for my own wounds and emotional scars, I did not possess the skills to view it any other way. I perceived it as a rejection. This is what I call unnecessary self-torment. I caused myself pain and anguish. This is what many of us do when we push our issues aside and never go back to heal them. They show up in many other areas, and we don't even make the connection.

If I had not started doing the work needed to heal my own feelings of abandonment, I would have been absolutely debilitated when my children grew up and started moving away from home. In most cases, this is what parents long for. But when you are a wounded mother with abandonment issues, you fear the day the kids will leave you. My oldest daughter, Joi, knew the day she left for college would be a difficult one, and she knew she didn't have the patience or the time to coddle me through the ordeal, so she left while I was at work. If I had not begun the work of understanding how my past caused me to react, I would have thought it was the cruelest thing a child could do to a parent. But because I was healing, and I understood her wanting to avoid a sad, drama-filled scene, I knew it was best. She was right to not allow me a long, drawn-out emotional goodbye that I would have still viewed as some form of abandonment.

When the healing process begins, you no longer view everything as an attack against you. Your perspective widens to accommodate the feelings and points of view of others.

I continued working on myself. I continued putting myself first. Today, I have healed many of my wounds. I used to call them "holes," which we all have. Some are larger than others. Today, at age fifty-four, many of the gigantic "holes" left from the hurt and abuse that I walked around with are closed. I know I'm worthy of love and happiness, no matter how my life began. But that healing didn't drop out of the sky. I had to seek it out. I had to desire to stop viewing the world as horrid and me as its victim. I had to choose to stop being angry that I didn't have a perfect childhood. I had to forgive my parents for succumbing to their substance addictions.

Most importantly, I have to gain control over my thoughts. I had to practice replacing negative thoughts with positive ones, repeatedly until it became a habit. That is what I want each of you to do. Switching out the negative with the positive must become second nature to you. Your mind is the magical tool needed to transform your earthly experience into a happy, fulfilling one. We all deserve and can achieve happiness.

In two thousand twenty-four, I was determined to commit to memory of inspirational poems. For one, to stimulate and strengthen the fifty-four-year-old memory, lol. And secondly, to inspire myself from the great thinkers of the past. This is the first poem I learned:

> Out of the night that covers me,
> Black as the Pit from pole to pole,
> I thank whatever gods may be
> For my unconquerable soul.
> In the fell clutch of circumstance
> I have not winced nor cried aloud.
> Under the bludgeonings of chance

> My head is bloody, but unbowed.
> Beyond this place of wrath and tears
> Looms but the Horror of the Shade,
> And yet the menace of the years
> Finds, and shall find, me unafraid.
> It matters not how strait the gate,
> How charged with punishments the scroll,
> I am the master of my fate:
> I am the captain of my soul.

"Invictus" by Willam Ernest Henley (1849-1903)

Become better for yourself and no one else. Live for you; let every day's mission be for you to feel happiness and peace in every moment. You are the captain of your soul. Your fate lies in your own hands. When you don't feel great, learn the tools to analyze and process the emotions, then release them and move forward. As long as you are alive, there will always be something that has the potential to cause you pain. Small, daily negative situations at home and work can, if you allow them to, chip away at your happiness and peace. Acknowledge your feelings in every moment, learn from them, and proceed with life with your new tools. Customize your tools for your life. Create personal affirmations specifically for your needs and the areas you want to improve. Throughout your daily life, you will have to pull many of those tools out of the toolbox to navigate through life and stay positive. Some of the transformational work may seem repetitive and tedious but don't give up. Repetition is necessary to reprogram the mind. Commit the positive tools to habit, and soon you will rejoice in the evidence that they work. You will see positive changes in your life and mindset.

One Christmas, I was working a little harder than usual because we had just had some construction done on the house and we had an upcoming cruise to Belize to pay for by Christmas Day. On this day, I worked for eight hours, ran to pay bills after work, and grabbed a few Christmas gifts for my two daughters, who were still living at home. By the time I arrived home, it was dark, and I was tired and hungry.

I came into the house and asked my adult daughter, "Hey, what's for dinner?"

She smiled and said, "We already ate."

She had ordered a pizza for her and her little sister. It instantly hurt my feelings that I had done so much to ensure a good Christmas and a comfortable home for them, and they did not even think of me and what I would eat after a long workday.

I glanced at my daughter and silently took myself and my hurt feelings into my home office. By this age, I had long since passed the shouting and blowing-up phase of my life. We are responsible for how we respond to others. Even though I felt justifiably hurt, I didn't express how selfish and ungrateful I thought she was. While in my office, I put on my Tibetan flute music, closed my eyes, and began to remind myself how unselfish my daughter is ninety-eight percent of the time. I chose to remember the positive times and not judge her on this one incident. She should have made sure I had something to eat and not carelessly brushed it off. However, this is exactly what this book is about—how to stay positive in day-to-day situations. I calmed my spirit down, never said a word to her, and sat and thought about how helpful and kind she normally was around the house. How great of a big sister she is and how much we laugh and enjoy each other ever since she returned home. Because I raised her well, about an hour later, she came into my home office and said, "Mom, did I hurt your feelings?" I told her yes and very calmly explained why. She apologized. We hugged, kissed, and moved forward in love.

Yes, life is filled with many catastrophic incidents. Undeniable tragedies occur to many of us. However, in this book, I want you to realize the damage tiny, small daily situations can have on your life. Every moment you hold on to anger and resentment, you are endangering your mind and body. "Perfectly Positive" was written to bring your attention to the smaller moments that we allow toxicity into our lives and the harm it does overall.

One day, after a weekend of events and commitments, I was finally coming from the last event, which I took a Lyft to because I was tired and I don't like to drive at night. I was grateful that I had made it to this event because Natalyn Randle, the founder of "Black Business Women Rock," is someone that I admire and consider a friend. However, by the time I got into the Lyft, I was exhausted. The man driving instantly caught my attention with his bright smile and charming personality which was apparent as soon as I buckled my seatbelt and looked up at him. I don't remember exactly how it began, but five minutes into driving, we engaged in a deep conversation about my favorite subjects: metaphysics, religion, spirituality, and the power of the mind. I instantly lit up. I love people who can converse on subjects beyond the surface. We talked all the way home. When he found out I was an author of self-help books, he was intrigued. He expressed interest in wanting to continue the conversation and telling me more about what he believed in since I pretty much monopolized our first conversation. I was ecstatic about the idea because it is extremely rare to meet people who can engage in discussions about the exact topics that I am passionate about.

    I gave him my business card and got out of his car. He said that he would text me right away so I could also have his phone number. The next day, I was busy at the salon, but I did notice that he had not texted me as he said he would. I went on working and didn't think about it again for a few days.

    By the end of the week, I thought of him again, and I remember feeling a little disappointed that he had not contacted me. I wanted to keep the knowledge flowing, and I had no way of contacting him. There is nothing more stimulating to me than a person who has deep thoughts and ideas and wants to acquire extended knowledge about the human life experience.

On day four or five, he finally texted me and said he was looking forward to speaking with me again. He asked me if I believed in "soul mates." I told him that I did and said we would speak soon.

Maybe a day or so after that, early one morning, I called. He didn't answer, so I left a voicemail, reminding him who I was and jokingly said, "Great people like us usually rise early."

He called back around 9:45 a.m. I was excited to have this deep conversation, but he told me, "My full voice doesn't come in until later in the day."

I thought that was the most ridiculous thing I had ever heard, but my reply was a simple, "Interesting."

He asked, "What do you mean by 'interesting'?"

I told him, "People who evolve to our level understand the importance of seizing the moment."

We spoke briefly about reading, which is a deep passion of mine. "What is the last book you read," I asked him, and his answer was vague. I was ready with pen in hand to write the author's name down, but he could not seem to give me a straight answer.

"In the afternoon, my head will be clearer," he said, asking if we could talk later when his "full voice" was in and his thought pattern was clearer. I reluctantly agreed and ended the call.

I immediately realized he wasn't the great, knowledgeable, evolved person that I assumed he was from our first conversation. I was quite disappointed—a little too disappointed for my taste.

He was technically a stranger. I texted him and told him I was not interested in speaking later and that I had put him on a pedestal from day one that he did not deserve to be on. I expressed that now that I was aware he was not this mini guru or this great "seize the moment" being, I was no longer interested in speaking to him again. Now, I know that was mean, but that was precisely where the true work began. Why was I so disappointed by a man I barely knew? What information was I yearning to hear or learn that I was crushed he didn't have? It truly wasn't about him. It was about me and what my soul was yearning for—this great hidden knowledge that I felt I was being called to uncover. At that moment, I had to internalize my response and determine what the true root of it was—I was hungry for knowledge. The answers to the true mysteries of the world, and our mere conversation during my car ride home gave me hope that ancient wisdom was near. This man got pulled into something that had absolutely nothing to do with him. I had elevated him to guru status. I still think the "full voice until the afternoon" excuse was strange, but I created a situation of letting myself down. It forced me to dissect my feelings and analyze why a stranger I had come in contact with for less than thirty minutes could cause me great disappointment—so much so that this stranger, whose name was Mike Everrt, earned this section in the book.

I'm still unpacking that one, but maybe certain people trigger us in areas that we still need to work on. We are supposed to cross paths with certain people for a reason. My desire for truth and knowledge about mankind and the universe is still great, but maybe the lesson does not lie within another human being. Maybe the answers are within me and have been all along. Perhaps I thought he knew the truth about alien existence, the construction of the Pyramids of Giza, or other mysteries of the universe. I was hoping he could enlighten me with some ancient wisdom about our true existence. Who knows? What I learned is that I definitely could have handled that with more love and compassion. I also learned to stop looking for people to give me what I have the power to create for myself. What we seek is seeking us, and we will find it.

CHAPTER 8

When "Just Pray About It" Is Not Enough

If you have ever been a member of any religious community, you know that the most common instruction given to those in distress is "Just pray about it." Although many of us love and honor God, when we are depressed, hurting, or grieving we need practical day-to-day tools to help us recover from the pain that we are in. During the worst times of our lives, "Just go pray about it" can seem dismissive. I have spoken to so many people who felt they could not get the help they needed when they came to their spiritual leaders for mental and emotional help. I believe in prayer. My prayerful C.O.G.I.C grandmother raised me to pray. However, during some of the darkest days of my life, I found myself in need of more. Being cast away with only the instruction to go pray about it did not arm me with any guaranteed assistance. It made me feel that if my pain did not soon subside, then my faith in God just wasn't strong enough. Which caused more hurt combined with feelings of failure. I was never taught that I had any power or control over my suffering. Well, we do have power. God gave it to us. Even though you have heard this many times from me, I must say it again. It all starts in the mind. When the pain begins to decrease, it isn't always that something happens or that enough time passes. It can also be that you change the way you view the situation that hurt you so badly. That perception is changed in only one place—the mind. Mind is all.

You must learn practical daily tools to use in your life to help you uplift yourself and stay positive. You must be taught to stop saying phrases like "There is glory in suffering," "My head is killing me," "Lord, I don't have to be rich, just provide me with enough," and "God what happens to me here, I can bare as long as I have assurance of eternal life." Stop speaking sickness, poverty, death, and despair over your own life. Stop believing that it's okay to suffer through this life experience as long as you go to heaven when you die. Hear me clearly—you do not have to suffer. You can be happy, healthy, and prosperous. You are great and the words that come out of your mouth must represent that greatness. The thoughts that you focus on must represent that greatness. You must think the absolute best of yourself and believe you deserve all the goodness this world has to offer. You have the right to expect the best. You are worthy of the Best. We all are.

Yes, I believe prayer is essential. However, it must be an effective prayer. Not prayers of begging and wishing and hoping that one day God will help you. Speak it and claim it was already done. Thus, your prayer should be one of thankfulness for the healing, thankfulness for the job, etc. It's already done. Even before it materializes. I know it may be a new concept for many, but it is the very concept that will change your life. You must believe in things unseen as if they are already here. That changes the game tremendously. Hebrews 11:1 says, *"Now faith is the substance of things hoped for, the evidence of things not seen."* Please keep this in mind when you pray. It is not easy, but you must act as if the blessing has already materialized. Retrain your mind and pretend that you have already been granted the desires of your heart. Try to generate the emotions of gratitude that you would feel even though you cannot see the blessing yet. It's a mindset, but it works.

You are not a sinner trying to earn your way into God's good graces. You are a phenomenal creation of the almighty divine source that is perfect from the day of birth. You already possess the power inside of you to have all that you desire. The kingdom of heaven lies within you. Use your mouth to speak that powerfully. Affirmations are the key to creating the life you desire. Speak positive affirmations aloud and silently and attempt to create an internal mental picture of what you want.

Your affirmations should sound like this:
I am Great and Powerful.
I can do All things.

Perfectly Positive

All things are possible.
I am Happy, Healthy, and Whole.
My Mind is Strong and Expansive.
My Life is Abundant.

They should not sound like this:
Father, if You believe I am worthy, may I please be blessed?
God, please. May I own a home?
Lord, will You one day allow me to be Happy?
God, if you see fit, will You bless me with a husband?
Father, will You please cure me if You feel I deserve healing?

No! This represents lack and limitation and wishing, wanting, and hoping. God has already given you the power to call all of these things into existence. I realize it may not be easy to be grateful for something you have yet to see, but this is the key. You call it forth with your thoughts and your words. Then ultimately allowing yourself to feel that it's already done. The kingdom of heaven is already inside of you. You don't have to beg God for anything. Believe that it is already yours and watch it show up. Learn to command things into your reality. It is your birthright to live in perfect health and abundant wealth. Adopting this frame of mind is not easy and will require you to reprogram your mind, but this is the key to success in all areas of your life. If you believe in the concept of prayer, then you cannot deny that you have never seen a "Prayer." You have never physically seen a prayer floating by or up into the heavens. Which means it is an unseen energy force. Ponder that for a moment and realize that you already can believe in things unseen. You already can feel emotions that you cannot see with the physical eye. Could it be that the truly significant forces that have the power to transform our lives are indeed unseen? God is unseen. Much time and consideration should be given to cultivating the unseen powers within us. We can express love physically, but the emotion of love itself is unseen. We can physically express happiness, but feeling happiness is unseen. When we sit and meditate, we are shutting out all the tangible things around us, turning within ourselves to focus on the unseen.

Subconsciously, we know the importance of the energies that we cannot see. I believe a happy life starts from the inside out. Let your prayers represent the knowledge that you know you are great and worthy of all that you are asking God for. Simply tweak your prayer from pleading and begging to gratitude and thankfulness. Because it's already done. All possibilities already exist. You simply have to learn to vibrate at the same frequency they are on. Start by saying it repeatedly. This practice will help you to begin to believe it. Limitations are not real. Shoot for the star because the world is yours if you desire it.

Don't allow other people to dissuade your faith. People can discourage you with phrases such as "That's not possible" or "You're asking for too much. Come on now." Sit with yourself quietly and refine in detail precisely what it is that you desire. Be consistent and try not to waiver. Don't say negative self-sabotaging things. Speak as if the home, spouse, job, car, etc., is already yours. Try to generate a sincere feeling of gratitude. Bask in that amazing feeling. Close your eyes and visualize all the things you desire. Allow your mind to dismiss any doubt and fear and soon you will see it in the physical form. That rule applies no matter who you are or what religion you follow. The amazing divine source created us in his image as one collective consciousness, but each person must individually tap into the greatness within them. It's time we all remember the wonderful powers God has bestowed upon us all. Life is to be lived to the fullest, but only you have the power to create that for yourself.

Prayer is indeed essential, but it must be effective prayer. If you do not believe that what you are asking God for is possible, it won't be. I understand that in a world of seemingly obvious limitations, it may be hard to conceptualize the idea that all things are possible, but they are. All things! There is no house too big, no salary too large, no degree of happiness too great for you to have. The object is knowing precisely how to bring it to fruition.

Learning to craft your prayers in a way that eliminates fear and doubt is the key. Believe it and you shall receive it!

CHAPTER 9

Vibrate High

By 2023, the phrase "vibrate high" or "raise your vibration" had become quite popular. To understand what it means to vibrate high, you first have to learn and accept that we are all vibrational beings. There is an unseen energy radiating through and around us all. When looking at or touching a human being, it does not seem that they are vibrating, but they are. All things are vibrating. Nothing is solid. We are not just matter; we are energy itself. Energy is constantly evolving. Nikola Tesla once said, "If you want to find the secrets of the universe, think in terms of energy, frequency, and vibration."

Often, when we have spent a lot of time monitoring our thoughts and taking control over our lives, it seems to cause us to be more in tune with the divine energy that surrounds and runs through us all. Whether you have gotten to the point in your life where you believe it or not, we are all energy. God is the supreme energetic source. He is not in physical form, but we are. In this human physical form, we have certain constrictions. However, as you become more in tune with the spiritual part of yourself, it becomes easier to understand that as an energetic being, even though we are confined to a physical body, we can still take control over the level of vibration we emit into the world. We are all vibrating at different frequencies. The goal is to be in control of whether you vibrate at a higher or lower frequency. When we are rushing, agitated, irritated, sad, fearful, or angry, we are vibrating at a lower frequency. No matter who you are—male, female, Christian, Catholic, Buddhist, adult, child, preacher, teacher, pilot, nurse, etc.—if you are walking around mad all the time, you are operating at that moment at a low vibration. Therefore, you will attract others that are also vibrating at a low frequency. For example, if you are annoyed and complaining at work all the time, somehow you will attract another employee who feels the same way. The two of you will become friends and will spend your time whining and complaining about working together. Like attracts like. However, people who are happy and optimistic and seem to be grateful for their jobs will attract others who are like them. This is because of the vibrational energy we all put out. The frequency you are on attracts others on the same frequency. Negative people usually surround themselves with other negative people and vice versa.

Based on my personal experience, I have noticed that in the hustle and bustle of our everyday lives, we often neglect to pause and truly connect with the frequencies and energies around us. However, once I started dedicating time to sit in stillness within a peaceful environment, and simply focus on my breath, observation, and listening, I became aware of the frequency I was emitting in that moment. Additionally, I learned how to alter it if it was on a lower scale. We focus on the seen and not the unseen. If I was mad and moving fast and thinking negatively, I learned to stop in my tracks and turn everything off—no TV, no cell phone, no radio. Just stop and ask myself, "What's wrong, SaBrina? Why are you mad? Who are you upset with? Who hurt your feelings?" I taught myself how to tap into the unseen forces, and you can too. God is an unseen divine force. The answer didn't always come instantly, but if I would just sit, breathe, and wait, I could usually identify the issue. It could be something truly simple. I could have had a conversation with someone that made me sad or mad. One of my children could have been acting spoiled or ungrateful, which always put me in a bad mood. A client at my salon could have been late and wasn't apologetic about it. Identifying what precisely is the problem helps you move past it. Dealing with it in your mind, then choosing to let it go, is one surefire way of raising your vibration or changing your mood—same difference. Changing our mood when we aren't in a good mood is very important. Taking steps to change your emotional state from sad to happy is "Raising Your Vibration." If we allow ourselves to stay in that negative headspace, we will attract more and more negativity, and the people who are at that same low vibrational level will gravitate to us.

When our lives are super busy, it's difficult to steal away and find moments to be still. Once you search for those moments of peace, you see that even for the busiest of people, there are always five minutes of spare time somewhere throughout the day. Even if it's staying an extra five minutes in the bathroom stall or not starting the car up right away when you leave work or home, just sit there and take deep breaths. Assess how you are feeling. Check in with yourself. You are the most important person in your world, and it is time to act like it. We all forget to attend to our own needs first. We must take care of our own mental and emotional needs before anyone else's. Allowing ourselves a mere few minutes for a vibrational self-check can improve our lives tremendously. After we attend to ourselves first, only then can we be a better parent, friends, co-workers, spouses, etc. We spend countless hours attending to the needs of others and rarely stop to check in with ourselves. Use this new tool you are learning from reading this book and start with yourself. Show the most love and concern for yourself first. It will change your life for the better.

I have created many personal spaces in my home and workplace for quiet. I have a meditation/prayer area at work and home. In those spaces, I have many vibrational tools such as sound bowls, rain sticks, gongs, and iPads, so I can play guided meditation videos or binaural beats. The one I listen to the most is 432 Hz. It's a beautiful, calming tone that settles my spirit and allows me to stay peaceful and positive. My second favorite is Tibetan flute music. There is an endless amount of this streaming on YouTube. Find tools that work for you. This is your world, and you come first. Create a world that allows you to operate at your very best. When we calm our spirits and take time to show love to ourselves, we find we become more creative. We become more patient and loving. Love and peace allow us to tap into the God within us all and get a clearer vision of our specific purpose here on Earth.

The daily goal is to Vibrate High—meaning, to be happy, healthy, and peaceful—not to operate with lower vibrational frequencies like hate, anger, pain, or fear. These low-vibrating frequencies can and will damage the quality of our lives. We can also transfer these negative energies to others. In this book, you will learn how to identify your mood or frequency. When you know that you are vibrating low, you must change it. Here are some examples of low vibrational thoughts and situations:

1. Arguing with someone
2. Road rage or driving impatiently
3. Speaking phrases like:
   - "I'm broke"
   - "I'll never find love"

- "I will probably die young"
- "No one loves me"
- "I will never find a job"
- "God is punishing me"
- "This world is horrible," etc.
4. Thoughts of suicide or harm to yourself or another
5. Hoarding money for fear of losing it
6. Speaking death, lack, and limitation over your life
7. Fears of all kinds
8. Judgment of others
9. Unfounded beliefs such as:
    - A: "My parents died of cancer, so I know I will too."
    - B: "Rich people are evil and can't make it into heaven."
    - C: "My mother was an alcoholic, so it's in my bloodline."
    - D: "We must suffer in life to be strong," etc.

While all of this may seem nonsensical, it is important to acknowledge that millions of individuals sincerely believe that they are fated to experience terrible circumstances in life. I used to believe that way as well. We do not have to suffer for the sins of our mothers and fathers, nor do we have to accept all of their lifelong fears as our own. We do not have to be destined to die of the same diseases as our ancestors. We possess the key to creating the life we desire through our thoughts and imagination. The power lies with us and us alone. The true power lies in how high or low we choose to vibrate. Your manifestation depends on your vibration. Use this internal power to think of happiness, good health, and wealth. Allow that positive thinking pattern to become a habit, and just watch how your life will change for the better.

For many years, when I was in my twenties and thirties, I had thoughts of suicide. After losing the grandmother who raised me from three months to seventeen years old to a violent crime, I was done with the world. I wanted to die.

My grandfather, the husband of my father's mother, took my grandmother's life in front of me in May 1987 when I was seventeen years old. It was my last year of high school. I was the captain of the varsity cheerleading team at Centennial High School in Compton, California. I was dating Clyde Arnold Reece, the man who eventually became my first husband and father to my only son, Justin Clyde Reece.

I lived in Compton on 126th Street with my grandparents and my older sister, Mary. My sister and I were only a year apart, and we were the only children of my grandmother, Ella Mae Fisher Fair's youngest son, Jesse Paul Fisher. My grandmother and her second husband moved to California with her three children from Dallas, Texas—Charles Edwin Fisher, SaBra Scott Fisher (who I was named after), and Jesse Paul Fisher (my father)—for a better life.

Our grandmother took us in at three and eleven months

old because our mother was an addict and incapable of raising us. Our father lived with us, but his mother, our grandmother, was our primary caregiver. She was a godsend. She loved us and raised us lovingly as her own. Everything that an old-school Texan grandmother could have taught you, we learned.

We washed socks by hand on a washboard and hung them on the line in the backyard with wooden clothespins. We picked collard and mustard greens out of our backyard garden and learned the proper way to clean and cook them. We learned to honor and love God. We learned to respect our elders, speak only when spoken to, and move from in front of the TV because "our daddy was not a glass maker." Hahaha. We had a great childhood.

We saw no abuse in the home. That is why it was such a shock for our grandmother's life to be taken abruptly by her husband, our grandfather, McClendon Fair, whom we all called Mack. He was a tall, stocky, fair-skinned man who cut grass for a living. By the time my sister and I came to live with them, my grandmother and her husband were in their late sixties. It was a simple life. He provided for us all. There was no screaming or yelling of any kind in the home.

Suddenly, one day after a minor disagreement about church, he shot her in the head in our kitchen in front of me. They had been married for thirty-two years. It appeared to be a happy marriage or at least a peaceful one. Other than that, one disagreement over the church, I never once saw them exchange harsh words. I also witnessed no affection between them, either. Mack never kissed or hugged us, but he was not mean or cruel to us in any way.

We were not his blood. We were the daughters of his wife's youngest son. I don't believe he had any biological children. I don't remember him giving us advice or teaching us any life lessons. I don't remember him involving himself in our lives much at all. But I can say I felt no negativity from him. He never lost his temper, elevated his voice, or hit any of us. There had been no history of violence that would make what he did make sense.

This was the day my life changed. This is when I realized there was evil in the world and that evil does not always roar or give you warning signs. Writing this, I am reflecting on our lives before the murder and noticing that it was a simple, peaceful home until that fateful day in May 1987.

I don't know exactly what makes a simple man, a basic provider who enjoyed watching "Jeopardy!" with Alex Trebek nightly with his wife, suddenly snap and kill her. However, it happened, and my life was never the same because of it.

My grandmother was a loving, wonderful woman who sacrificed her elder years to raise two small babies. When she took my sister and me home to live with her, she was already sixty-six years old, and we were only eleven months and three months old—stair-step babies. She was a strict but kind, traditional Southern woman from Dallas, Texas, who taught us many priceless Southern values. We knew how to roll out biscuits from scratch, make salmon croquettes, and cook chicken and dumplings from scratch.

We had a normal, peaceful life. We skated and rode bikes with the other children in the neighborhood, specifically the kids who lived on 126th Street between Compton Avenue and Wilmington Avenue. I know we were not wealthy, but I do not believe we were poor. We were never hungry. Our refrigerator was never empty, and even a huge deep freezer stayed stocked. We had all our needs met.

We took piano lessons and had dolls, bikes, and skates like the other children on the block. As little girls, we played jump rope, jacks, and tetherball outside under a huge avocado tree in the backyard. We grew up in the Church of God in Christ (C.O.G.I.C.) and became members of the Sunday School and Usher Board. My grandfather never attended church with us, but he didn't seem to mind us going. That was something only my sister, my grandmother, and I did.

There was nothing that my sister and I ever saw growing up that would have given us any sign that our grandfather was capable of killing our beloved grandmother. Yet in May 1987, he shot her in the head, and she died instantly. At this early stage of my life, I had never heard of such tragedies. In 1987, we watched television shows like "The Brady Bunch," "I Love Lucy," "One Life to Live," and "General Hospital." I did not know tragedies of this sort even happened in the world.

Losing her in such a tragic way was devastating. Witnessing it as a seventeen-year-old caused irreparable damage to my soul. One month after her murder, I attended my high school graduation from Centennial High School in Compton, California. I am one hundred percent sure I did not complete all of my work that year. The teachers were all made aware of the tragedy, and I was not required to do the make-up work. A lot of those immediate days after losing my grandmother are still a blur. I don't know how I got up each day.

Our father had died of alcohol-related illnesses when my sister and I were only ten and eleven years old. Our mother, Shirley Ann Tillman, was still heavily active in her drug addiction. And now our grandmother, the one person who loved us as her own when our biological mother could not, was gone, leaving me with the image of her being shot to death forever ingrained in my mind. There is no lower vibration than that. The dark energy that must have been floating around our house that day in Compton was apparent.

My grandfather was not a spiritual man. We all must learn that when negative thoughts come your way when you are at your lowest mentally and emotionally, do not allow those negative thoughts to consume you. Realize in those moments that you do not have to listen to those negative thoughts or comply with anything they are telling you to do. Learn tools to elevate your mindset instantly. Do not give in to the darkness.

I tell you this story to show how many horrible situations in life affect the way we think and view the world regarding "Low Vibrations." On that horrid day, there could not have been any lower or darker energy circulating. When someone takes the life of another, they are in a dark place. They are, and most likely have been, vibrating dangerously low for a long time. Although it ended in tragedy for my family, it does not have to end in death and doom for everyone. If you learn to change your frequency and pull yourself from darkness into the light, you can avoid tragedy.

I'm not saying that victims are responsible for the horrendous things that happen to them. We exist in a world where good and bad exist, and there seems to be nothing we can do about it. The only control we have is over ourselves. We can do our best to elevate our vibration and stay as positive as possible. We must learn to sit, be still, and do a "Self Check." Acknowledge harmful feelings, assess the cause, and attempt to change them. No, positivity is not perfect. It takes consistent work. However, the positive energy that we exude will rub off on others, and that can lead to a better world.

I know people reject all the vibration talk and dismiss it as "New Age" lingo, but there is nothing new about it. From the beginning of creation, energy has always been a factor. We simply did not learn about it. We, as a human race—more so, Americans—never knew about energy and vibration and how to manipulate and manage it. Every object has vibrations. Having traveled to multiple countries, I have noticed that most people not only acknowledge the existence of this potent energy but it is also passed down to them by their ancestors and plays a significant role in their cultural beliefs.

All that you believe is solid is not. Everything is energy operating at different frequencies.

I can't say that I fully understand how energy works, but I have experienced many unexplainable, unseen events. One day, I had an appointment with a woman named Orly in North Hollywood, California.

Orly is a spiritual therapist who specializes in Past Life Regression. This was a subject that I had casually studied over the years. I finally decided that I wanted to have a past life hypnosis session specifically to see if Phillip Clarence Morris, aka Diablo, my youngest child's father, and I had a connection in a past life. As I mentioned in my first two books, I had a very hard time moving on from him, even though I knew he wasn't the man I deserved. Because I kept reentering my involvement with him, I truly wanted to know what my problem was. I was a strong, powerful woman in every other area of my life—a woman who led others and had absolutely no problem speaking her mind to anyone and everyone but him. I had convinced myself that the unbreakable tie must be spiritual.

I arrived at my appointment, excited and a little apprehensive. Orly and I sat and spoke about my life and my history with my daughter's father for over an hour, which made me more comfortable. Finally, it was time for her to hypnotize me. I asked her if I could go to the bathroom first. I believe I was a little nervous. I returned from the bathroom, and she said, "Are you ready?" I said yes, but I quickly grabbed my cell phone to see if anyone had called or texted since I would be under for over an hour. When I looked at my phone, I had a text from Phillip, my daughter's father. The very person I was there to be hypnotized about, and the text read "Ready."

I absolutely could not believe it. He and I had not spoken in over three days. We were not meeting up that day for any reason, and there was no reason for him to be texting me the word "Ready." He did not know I was about to be hypnotized to fully understand and get over our strange, unhealthy entanglement. What the heck was that? Were we truly connected spiritually? How in the world was he asking if I was ready? The exact phrase that Orly had just asked me, and he did not know that I was in North Hollywood, about to be hypnotized to find out why I was so deeply connected to him. He and I were not in the middle of a dialogue or text thread.

I was so stunned by this I had to tell Orly about it. She, of course, believes strongly in these energetic connections, so it wasn't a surprise to her and she told me it was very possible that somehow, he felt what was happening. Maybe not in detail, but energetically, he felt something. I still don't even know what he was asking me if I was "Ready" for. When I texted back, he never replied. Meaning, what else could this be but energy and vibration? I laid down to be hypnotized.

Orly took me back to a life years ago when I was an Asian girl raised in poverty by her father. I married a man who was the owner of a newspaper company. We had one son. I remember seeing the dresses of the olden times and the cars from many years ago. I had a hard time distinguishing my memory from my imagination. I strongly believe in the concept of humans living multiple lives, also known as reincarnation. However, I had some doubts about whether I was under hypnosis.

I kind of felt like I was making it all up. I felt pressure to give her what she wanted.

I shared with Orly that I was uncertain that I was under, and she understood, but said it was too much detail. She said my story was so descriptive that she believed it was indeed a memory of a past life. I loved Orly and went back a second time, but this time, I only wanted spiritual counseling. I didn't see the need to do another past life regression at three hundred seventy-five dollars an hour, as I did not believe it was a past life regression. I take nothing away from Orly or her abilities. I simply felt like I may have been worried that I was the only person in the world that hypnosis wouldn't work on, so I imagined what I thought she may have wanted to hear.

Now, let me be clear, I am uncertain I made it up. I still remember every detail to this day. I may very well have recalled a past life. I am just not sure. Either way, it revealed nothing about why I was so strongly connected to Phillip Clarence Morris—why I couldn't completely break away from him and tell him to "Go to hell." We share a child—a

Perfectly Positive

beautiful, kind little girl named Journey Schy Morris, and before we conceived her, he and I were best friends for many years. I truly wanted to understand why he had such a huge presence in my life and a strong mental and emotional hold over me. Are we twin flames? Did we create irreversible soul ties somehow? Had we created soul contracts before we came to Earth? I was determined to figure it out so I could completely move on with my life and stop allowing him to drop into it whenever he felt like it.

I believe the reason I was so convinced it was a spiritual tie is because one day, after an intense disagreement with him, I came home and went to sleep very upset. That night, I dreamed of him. He was walking toward the door, leaving my bedroom, and he seemed as if his shoes were made of cement. He was struggling and appeared to be moving in slow motion to get to the door. Once he finally reached it, he touched the doorknob and looked back at me, and instantly a black spirit flew from his body onto mine. The spirit was heavy, and it had the entire left side of my body pinned down. I tried to speak, but the left side of my mouth was experiencing paralysis. Being raised a Christian, I attempted to do the only thing I knew how, which was to plead the blood of Jesus—speaking the words "The Blood of Jesus" with my mouth, quite literally. The first couple of attempts were hard because I was paralyzed, but I kept trying. By attempt number four or five, I screamed, "The Blood of Jesus," and the spirit lifted off my body and flew away.

It doesn't get more spiritual than that. To this day, I don't know exactly what that was or why it happened, but that incident made me believe that Phillip and I were spiritually connected, and I badly wanted to break that connection. I believe the black spirit that flew off of him was trying to tell me something, possibly warn me of something. I didn't believe it was real. As soon as I formed that question in my mind, the spirit took me by the arm and said, "Bri, no." That's it, no other words. No "What?" Mr. Spirit, I need clarity. Maybe our daughter has a great purpose on this earth. Possibly we had to connect to bring her into the world. If so, why did our connection have to be so toxic? Why was his nickname Diablo? Had I been sleeping with the devil? And if so, how could we create such a beautiful, kindhearted child? Who knows, but I was adamant that I would not write about him again. Yet here we are in book number three, in 2024, and he and I still have not fully broken our connection. He is fifty-seven, and I am fifty-four, and we still find ourselves gravitating back to each other physically. I have yet to understand why.

I tell you that story to get you to understand that there are unseen energies. There are low-vibrating beings that exist. There is value in intentionally vibrating high. Use whatever tools work for you to raise your energetic vibration. When we vibrate low, we attract all things at that same level of vibration, such as sickness, disease, depression, anger, poverty, etc. When we vibrate high, we attract happiness, prosperity, love, kindness, peace, etc. We can individually change our frequency. Even though there are people and situations that we have no control over, we can choose how we react. We can do our best, no matter what, to vibrate higher, even amid chaos.

When you are upset, take a moment for yourself and breathe, calm down, and elevate your vibration. That may be simply by telling yourself, "Everything will be okay and all things work out for the good." That one works for me. All things do indeed work out for the good, but you must believe and trust in that possibility.

I sit still and meditate to keep myself peaceful. Meditation is a tool that allows you to tap into and feel the energy flowing through you. Learning to meditate takes dedication. Do not give up when it seems you can't sit still or that your mind is steadily wandering. You will get better at it and eventually see the benefit of quieting the mind, body, and soul. It will teach you how to process precisely what you are feeling. If those feelings are not serving you well, through meditation, you can change them.

When we are angry, we can't think straight. We can't find a positive solution to the problem when we are mad. I assure you, that no matter how dark and hopeless a situation may be, there is a higher vibratory way to handle it. Choosing to approach all situations from a higher mindset will benefit us all in the long run.

We lower our vibration by entertaining thoughts that are

not even true. When we believe someone does not like us and then hold negative feelings inside of us about ourselves then we could be wrong. Whether they like us is not our business, and their feelings should not affect our internal vibration. They are fighting their own spiritual battles that have nothing to do with us. We have to learn to turn inward, love ourselves, trust our instincts, and follow the vibrations that feel good to us. We must resist taking everything personally, or we will be miserable, and our vibration will drop low. When it drops low, guess what happens? More low-vibrational things come our way.

The biggest takeaway that I would like you to receive from this book is to learn how to vibrate higher. You are in control of your energy. It is your job and no one else's to make sure you maintain a high vibration. It is okay to eliminate people from your life who consistently vibrate low. These people are not evil; they just have not figured out how to manage their vibration. They do not know that they are in control of their feelings, their energy, and their emotions. They are miserable and have not yet been given the tools to elevate themselves. It is okay to love them from a distance until they do the necessary work to elevate their life vibration. It is not your job to be weighed down by their misery.

You are responsible for you. Make choices that create high vibrations for yourself. If you choose to be around a person who makes you feel bad, that is exactly what will happen. If you choose to be around a person who makes you feel happy and good, that is exactly what will happen. Learn to pay close attention to how you feel in any given moment, and any particular environment, and do more of what makes you feel good. Listen to more music, dance in the mirror, take yourself on a shopping spree, watch funny movies, walk in nature, smell the flowers, and hug a tree. Your vibration is a choice, and you get to choose the level of your vibration. Choose to vibrate higher in all that you do, and you will see your entire life elevate to new levels.

CHAPTER 10

You Win The War—The World Is Yours

It's time to celebrate your new life where you are the master of your fate! Learning how to control your thoughts is the catalyst to that. This is the beginning of a great life. It's all uphill from here. If you utilize the positive mind tools I speak of in the book, you absolutely cannot fail. You can win the war against negative thinking every single time. You have a magnificent future ahead of you. I am excited for you. Let every new season in your life be a winning season. Winning the battle over negative thinking will be one of the most significant and useful skills to have mastered. It will change your life.

It's one thing to learn to win the war against negative thinking yourself. It is a whole different challenge to teach it to others. However, that is exactly what it will take in order for the generations that follow us to be empowered enough to make an impactful difference in the world. We must teach each child about the infinite power within themselves.

Perfectly Positive

I have four children who thankfully got to be around during my mindset transformation and reaped the benefits of having a person in the home with them daily who was attempting to master the practice of positive thinking, thus being able to teach it to them. I am certain that even during times when they appeared to be disinterested, the concepts and ideas still rubbed off on them a bit. Their wonderful, expansive minds are like soil. If we plant positive thoughts, ideas, and concepts into them regularly, they will eventually develop habitual behaviors that will make them better people. My children, as well as yours, will have to create their own path, but I pray that watching me diligently follow my path shows my children that it is possible. All things are possible.

At age fifty-four, I began painting again. I always had the desire and the talent to paint, but I was so busy running "Braids By SaBrina" and "A New Vision Dreadlock Studio" and teaching braiding and dreadlock classes that I simply did not have time to paint. I had literally forgotten that I loved painting. It was only when I slowed my life down that I remembered the things that I was truly passionate about and began painting again. I painted just for myself, and it was gratifying and peaceful.

One day, after watching a video of me painting on TikTok, a woman named Maria kept asking if she could buy one of my paintings. Since I had never even considered selling them, I told her no. She asked a second and maybe even a third time. Suddenly, a little light bulb turned on, and I agreed to sell her the painting. That was all it took for me to tap into that "Inspiration for creation" and turn my passion into profit.

I quickly created about fifteen paintings. I called them "Spiritual Art From My Heart." I created a website and all other social media forums, and Whoa La! A new business was born. In the first seven days, I had already sold four paintings. I shifted into the energy of what I call "Creation Mode." When in creation mode, ideas are constantly flowing freely. You can't sleep until you complete your new project or, as I sometimes say, "Until you give birth to the new idea." We have all felt the powerful energy of "Creation Mode," but sometimes our daily lives distract us from recognizing it.

I urge anyone who can identify when they are operating at a high level of vibration to seize those moments and try to zero in on what God is trying to tell you to create. This is the energy that builds businesses. It's the solution energy, where you will always seem to find the answer to whatever you are seeking. It's fast-paced and quick because it's passing through you. You must grab it and relish in the feeling. Write every thought down, and meditate more often when you are feeling this magnificent energy. It will not last. It is a fleeting energy, far too powerful to exist indefinitely.

This energetic zone is the epitome of what I mean by the title of chapter nine, "Vibrate High." It is God within you, pushing you towards your purpose. You will experience little bursts of it throughout your entire life. Use those to your advantage. All of us have something amazing that God wants us to bring to fruition.

Sometimes tragedy or challenging situations can invoke that creative energy as well. When my youngest daughter was ten years old, in the fourth and fifth grades, we had a situation where she was being bullied. It was quite hurtful because the other child was her best friend. Well, her BFF (Best Friend Forever), as they call it.

As soon as I became aware of the situation, I immediately contacted the school and the other child's primary parent. Unfortunately, the parent of the bully was dismissive and made excuses for her child's behavior. The mother seemed to be of a similar mindset. After several meetings with the school principal and the teachers and counselors at the school, I became extremely frustrated and concerned about my daughter's emotional stability. Although removing her from school was an option, I did not believe that would fix the problem. There are bullies everywhere—in schools, workplaces, and even in the home.

Out of my frustration, I decided to create a positive movement for children to teach them how to navigate negative conversations, how to uplift themselves and others, and how to gain the strength and courage to say, "No, you cannot treat me like that." We must teach our children that it is okay to speak up for themselves, even if they are afraid.

Three days into my daughter's fifth-grade year, I had an appointment with the school to further address the fact that bad behavior from the same female student in fourth grade had carried over and was already beginning in the fifth grade. I thought it was important for the principal and teachers to be informed about this, hoping that they would finally address the behavior of this specific child. My patience was wearing thin with the school, but since I agreed to meet them the next morning at 8:15 a.m., I sat down and tapped into that creative spirit of mine and created "The Positive Crew System."

My computer printer wasn't working properly, so I went across the street to my godmother's house to use her computer and printer. I made about eight copies and took them with me to school the next morning. I even made a mission statement and an oath for the children to learn. I videotaped my daughter and her friend reciting the oath. I even had my best friend's grandson make a video. It was a fun way to introduce positivity to elementary school-age children.

I am learning to be in tune with when the power of God moves through me. I recognize that amazing energy because when it is active, ideas are instantaneous. This is the oath I created in five minutes:

The Positive Crew Oath
I am part of the Positive Crew
And negativity, we just don't do!
We uplift ourselves and others

Perfectly Positive

Every day of the week
We only use nice words when we speak
I will be kind to every boy and girl
So, we all can have a better world

If I'm completely honest, I never had any strong urges to work with children. I love kids and even have plans to write a children's book, but I never felt compelled to create and design a motivational program specifically for kids before that day. That's why I believe it was God pushing me for another purpose He had for my life.

I went on to create a mission statement and a page filled with other ideas of what this newfound Positive Crew System could develop into. Bullying is a nationwide problem. Children can only benefit from learning to be kinder to each other. We have nothing to lose. "The Positive Crew System" will teach them specific short, memorable phrases to navigate out of negative, hurtful conversations. It will teach them how to choose to say something nice as opposed to something hurtful. It will make being positive a cool thing. The mental health of the little people we depend on to evolve humanity for the better is at stake.

The point of this story is to get you to understand that you must always stop, take a breath, and try to find the positive in all situations. I was mad and frustrated with the child and the school. Had I responded out of that anger and frustration, the school would have never let me in the door, let alone listened to my proposal for "The Positive Crew System."

Even when we practice maintaining positivity, the ups and downs of life can still affect us. Don't feel you have failed. Positivity is a daily practice. However, I believe that we all stand a better chance of this world changing for the better if we empower children while they are young and impressionable. They truly are our future, so let's make sure they grow up armed with the tools needed to win the wars they will encounter throughout their lives.

There will always be opportunities in life for you to choose positivity. We are human beings, so we will never be immune to feelings of hurt and disappointment. However, when we choose to handle them positively, we will find that each time we learn a lesson that will assist us in our own emotional evolution. We become better people when we learn to respond from a place of love. Love is our true nature.

Make no mistake, there are people who will challenge us. For example, I have a friend who is part of "The Order Of the Eastern Stars," an organization I am a proud member of. She and I clicked immediately. She is funny, and no matter how long we go without seeing each other, we always fall right back into hysterical laughter when we get together.

In February 2024, she came back to California to tend to her ailing mother's needs. We met up the next day at an event. I was thrilled, as usual, to see her. I ran straight to her when she entered the room and gave her a big hug. She instantly began comically insulting me. As we posed for a picture, she said, "Hold your stomach in." I said, "You hold yours in," which is something I would never say to anyone. As we were leaving, she hugged me and said, "Bye, Chunky," alluding to the fact that I had gained weight. This time, I simply said, "I look fabulous."

It absolutely hurt my feelings, but what was most hurtful was, as my two daughters and I drove home, my older daughter JJ said, "Don't let her hurt your feelings, Mom. She was being mean." I had no idea they heard her. I explained to them that no one, especially a friend whom I am first in line to support, should ever treat someone that way. She, too, had gained weight, but I would never have pointed it out to her or anyone.

I also should never have allowed her to pull me into that negativity. When I snapped back at her, "Hold your stomach in" comment with "Hold yours in, too," that was wrong and goes against everything I believe in. I realized at that moment that possibly our friendship had run its course. If I am honest with myself, she has always been that way. She has always been a mean girl. I loved her so dearly that I chose to ignore it. But at this stage in my life, I was not willing to allow anyone to insult me.

Absolutely, I may have been extra sensitive because I had gained more weight than I desired. Maybe when I became her friend thirteen years earlier, I could engage in some negative conversations about others with her. But I was no longer that person. I had grown past that level of immaturity and was proud of my growth. I had won the war against the enemy of my mind. It saddened me that she still had not at sixty years old. However, we all have our own journeys. We all evolve at different paces.

She did call me about an hour later, but she was completely oblivious to the fact that her words were hurtful. I told her that my daughters heard her and had to comfort me when they realized her words hurt my feelings. She brushed it off by saying, "Girl, I talk about myself being fat all the time." No accountability whatsoever. I was a little sad because I knew it would be the end of the friendship as we once knew it. I'll always be cordial, and we may exchange a laugh or two when she comes to town, but that will be it. And that is okay. We can indeed love people from a distance. Every hurtful situation does not have to result in a negative confrontation.

I would not want my daughters to allow any friend to treat them that way. I wish her the absolute best in life, and I'm trying hard not to judge her because this is not new behavior for her. However, it is behavior I refuse to tolerate from anyone, especially from those who claim to love me. Friends uplift and encourage each other. Friends don't take potshots at each other for laughs.

There was a time when I was so broken that I would never have had the strength to distance myself from a hurtful friend. I did not love myself wholeheartedly then.

I'm not mad at my friend. I love her to this day. I pray for her regularly, but the only person that can change her is her. That holds true for each one of us. If there are behaviors or personality traits that you are not proud of, change them. Only you can create a better you. Each of us individually working on ourselves leads to humanity as a whole changing for the better collectively.

I have spent numerous years fighting the mental enemy that made me question my worth. Those days are over. I am great, and so are you. I have won the war, and you can win it too. There is no greater feeling than sincere, authentic self-love.

The world is yours. You have the power to design it any way that you want with your thoughts and imagination. Use your beautiful mind to create heaven here on Earth.

I am creating a world of love, respect, and peace for myself. When I close my eyes and imagine, I see a life filled with people who sincerely love me and always have my best interests at heart. Each of you can create the same for yourselves. We do not have to suffer during this life experience. Happiness is possible for us all.

We cannot rid the world of negative people—they will always exist—but we can limit access to anyone who is not radiating kindness and love. You have the starring role in your story. Take control over how your life turns out. Leave nothing to chance.

Implement the positive practices you have learned in this book and begin to enjoy everything that this amazing world has to offer. You can't change the chaos in the world, but you can learn to calm the chaos in your mind. In the endless battle of negative and positive, take purposeful steps to ensure that you win the war every time!

www.ingramcontent.com/pod-product-compliance
Lightning Source LLC
Chambersburg PA
CBHW060357080526
44583CB00012B/349